RIGS & END TACKLE

DEDICATION

To the memory of the master angler – Richard Walker.

Published by
Paisley-Wilde Publishing Ltd
1 Grosvenor Square, Sheffield S2 4MS

First published in 1991 by
Paisley-Wilde Publishing Ltd.
1 Grosvenor Square,
Sheffield S2 4MS

British Library Cataloguing in Publication Data

Alan Tomkins
End Tackle and Rigs
1. Carp Angling
1 Title
799. 1'752

ISBN 1 871700 15 9

Produced, Typeset and Published by
Paisley-Wilde Publishing Ltd.

Printed by
Gibbons Barford Print Ltd.

Acknowledgements

To my lovely wife Gill for putting up with a part-time husband each summer, and for dedicating one of the kitchen cupboards to my use, even if she does keep nicking my eggs!

For supplying me with various items of tackle, and generally being helpful, I am indebted to the following:

Alan Bramley of Partridge of Redditch
Terry Eustace
Kevin Nash
Pete Drennan
Richard Gardner of Gardner Tackle
Keith Selleck of the Middlesex Angling Centre
Dave Chilton of Kryston
John Roberts
Vic Bellars of Marvic
E.T. Products
Mustad

For allowing me to use previously unpublished pictures of carp caught on various rigs many thanks to: Gary Bond, John Miles, John Read

I would also like to thank various carp anglers whom I have met for their help over the years, among these Ritchie MacDonald who answered the many questions I put to him in the early 80's, a few years after I had returned to carp fishing following 10 years absence, enabling me to catch up on some of the developments I had missed in the 70's. To Chris Currie for putting me on to a winner at the start of the 80's. To Tim Paisley for his part in our somewhat erratic correspondence (his part was erratic, not mine) and again to Tim, and Bill Cottam of Nutrabaits for their help with bait. To Mike Wilson, a good angler, and a good friend, always ready to advise on any problem. To all the anglers I have fished with over the years (most of whom are called Steve or John!) I am grateful for their good company. Also to everyone who has ever written anything on carp fishing, because I will almost certainly have read it, and stored it in my brain somewhere. And finally, to anyone I have pestered with carp fishing questions over the years, including many anglers who are quite famous, none of whom have ever refused to give relevant advice and information (except Kevin Pembroke...!).

CONTENTS

Introduction

There was a time when a carp rig was simply a bait of some kind impaled upon a hook. To allow any part of the hook, except perhaps the very tip of the point, to protrude from your bait was anathema, and supposedly fatal to your chances of having it picked up by a carp. That it never made any difference when the hook necessarily protruded from such baits as worms and maggots didn't seem to deter the exponents of the hidden hook from burying it in their balls of bread paste, and par boiled potatoes. The only choice you then had to make was how much weight, if a weight was needed, you would need to cast out. The thinking then was to fish in such a way that the fish, on picking up the bait, encountered as little resistance as possible, so anglers either free-lined or used very small weights. I can remember only 10 or 11 years ago how incongruous a 1 oz. lead dangling from my Mk. IV seemed! I think it fair to say that the rig revolution has mainly come about in the last 10 years. Side-hooking and top-hooking were the first two breakthroughs, followed soon after by the hair rig. The use of heavier leads also became common, as anglers realised – initially – that a heavier lead which would not move offered less resistance on a running ledger, than a small lead which could go bouncing across the bottom as a carp moved off with the bait. It also, of course, enabled you to cast further. The so called 'self-hooking' rigs, usually fixed or back-stopped leads, or tightly clipped up lines, also came about at this time, and were, and still are, criticised by many for performing that function. I think though, if one is honest, one has to admit that many rigs are self-hooking whether it has been intended or not, and I do not regard such criticism as valid. Where, for instance, is the skill in striking a full blooded carp run? And if you are having to strike at twitches, then you have possibly got something wrong anyway. Though I don't know who first realised the fact, probably the most important discovery of all was the realisation that carp were capable of differentiating between the hookbaits and the free offerings. This was an absolute revelation, and produced a flood of ideas designed to fool the carp into thinking the hookbait was not attached to anything. In its original form the hair-rig began to take waters apart: carp, it seemed, were catchable. This one development is probably responsible for around 80% of the carp anglers you see fishing today being there. (Bait development has also had a hand of course, though this is not within the scope of this book). There have been countless variations on that single theme of separating the bait from the hook, and most, for a time at least, have been successful. Though I don't think the hair was originally conceived as an anti-eject rig, it soon became apparent that in the early days at least, it performed that function very efficiently. This sent carp anglers off on yet another tack. And once the hair got anglers thinking about end tackle, for a while hardly a week seemed to pass without a new rig being invented. Having developed the hair possibly to its fullest extent, carp anglers then began having problems with carp picking up the bait in their lips. With the bait attached to a hair, the fish weren't getting the hook in their mouths. This led anglers to turn their attention back to side-hooking, fine tuning the basic principles and developing such rigs as the swimmer rig, and the brilliant bent hook, in an effort to ensure that if a carp picked up the bait, it would also get the hook into its mouth, with every chance of the hook finding a hold. I know there are anglers who are now going back to the no resistance methods, and even know some who are hiding the hook in the bait. So the wheel has turned full circle.

The carp angler now has the choice of many different set-ups, and a combination of bits from all of them. Most of this knowledge is available, though spread out over many publications, to anyone who cares to look for it. The purpose of this book is to put it all in one place. It is however important to bear in mind that many rigs were developed to overcome a specific problem (though I suspect in some cases that specific problem was a nasty letter from the bank manager!), and that in setting up a rig, you should always be aware of what you are trying to achieve. If you can observe the carp's behaviour in your waters, then you are lucky - you will learn more in half a day than anglers fishing murky waters may learn in 5 years. If you can't see the fish, then you must try to interpret the action you are getting. If you can't see the fish, and are getting no action at all, then it becomes a case of trial and error, and can become very difficult. In which case, I would advise you to persevere, do something you have confidence in, and don't read the weekly angling papers to see what everyone else is catching! Anyway, for those old enough to remember, catching difficult fish used to be what carp fishing was all about, didn't it?

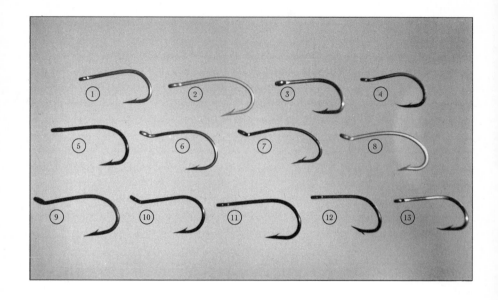

All size 4 unless stated

1. Drennan Super Specialist
2. Patridge Jack Hilton (Niflor coated)
3. Eustace Super Strong
4. Drennan Boilie Hook (6)
5. Patridge Record Breaker
6. Patridge JVB Solder Blob
7. Partridge KM Hair Rig Hook
8. Partridge Cassien Hook (Niflor coated)
9. Partridge Rod Hutchinson VW hook
10. Partridge Rod Hutchinson OW hook
11. Gardner (Partridge) Carp Hook
12. Partridge KM Outbarb
13. Au Lion D'or

HOOKS

Hooks; arguably the most important item of tackle, next to line. With those two we could catch fish. Without them, we couldn't. After all, what good is a £600 set of rods and reels without the relatively cheap hooks and line? In talking about hooks, I intend, in the main, to merely document the types available and briefly mention their advantages, and perhaps, disadvantages. Where I have practical experience of a particular hook I shall say so. I do think that life is too short for a carp angler to properly evaluate every hook on the market nowadays, and, like most carp anglers, I tend mostly to stick with the brands I have faith in.

I have no idea how many hook patterns there are on the market, but it must run into thousands. I have not the space to describe them all, so will put them into categories where common factors are apparent.

EYES

Starting at the blunt end - eyes, or lack of them, as the case may be. The main choice in eyed hooks is whether to choose up-eyes, down-eyes or straight-eyes. I really am not convinced that any one of these offers a great advantage over the others, except that some work better with some rigs than others. The type of eye may do two things – alter the angle of pull, or widen the hook gape. The angle of pull from a down-eyed hook will result in the hook being pulled in more in line with the point, and it may be less likely to pull out. It also closes the gape to some extent, and may prevent the hook becoming caught up in the carp's mouth in the first place.

The up-eyed hook does just the opposite – the angle of pull will be out of line with the point, and in theory the hook may be more liable to pull out, but the increased gap between point and tip of eye may help the hook to take an initial hold. The up-eyed hook is particularly useful in rigs such as the swimmer rig, where the bait is held tight to the back of the hook. Partridge's Rod Hutchinson OW and WW hooks are designed specifically for this rig, and have instructions on how to tie it, on the packet.

The straight-eyed hook sits somewhere in between the two, and if you're not sure which to choose, it offers a good compromise. Most anglers I know use straight-eyed hooks, except when they are using the bent hook, which I will come to later.

One thing worth mentioning about hook eyes is their size. Many anglers use knots that require two turns of the line to be passed through the eye. Some patterns have larger eyes than others, and therefore make it easier to use this type of knot. It may be a truism to say it, but hook eyes should be closed properly, especially if you are using multi-strand hook-links, which can squeeze through the smallest of gaps.

Then there are the spade-end and solder-blobbed hooks, which have no eye at all. The solder-blobbed hooks were used many years ago, as a result of strong hooks not being available for carp fishing. It was Jack Hilton who first started to use low water salmon fly hooks. These hooks do in fact have an eye, but it is what is termed in the trade as a loop-eye. A loop-eye is not closed at all, but after the metal is bent to form the eye, instead of being bent back almost full circle to form a closed eye, it continues parallel to the shank for about an eighth of an inch, and is not attached at all. These hooks are intended for dressing salmon flies on, and in that application the eye is closed up by the whipping silk. Though I have used these hooks for dressing salmon flies myself, I must admit I can see no reason for this peculiar arrangement. One could close the eye by this means for carp fishing, but it is a rather clumsy arrangement. What Jack Hilton did was to cut off the eye completely, then affix a blob of solder in its place. The hook was then tied on as a spade end, was used to great effect by anglers at that time, and was the forerunner of the still popular Jack Hilton carp hook. As well as still making the Jack Hilton hook, Partridge now make a solder blobbed hook if you wish to try one without having to fiddle about with soldering irons.

Correctly tied spade end with

line passing under the spade

The Kinryu spade-end.

I have to admit to a great distrust of spade end hooks, or at least the methods of attachment. It worries the life out of me that the edge of the spade just might cut through the line when a big fish is being played. I have spoken to anglers who regularly use spade ends, and they tell me if the hook is tied on correctly, that is with the line coming from under the upturned spade, then there is no danger of the line being cut. Perhaps I am subconsciously using my fear as an excuse because don't I fancy tying them on! I'm also aware that some anglers consider that the spade offers an advantage because, having no knot at the 'eye', it holds the hook in line with the hook-link better than an eyed pattern. This may be so with stiff hook-link materials, but I doubt it makes much difference with the almost universally used supple ones. If you do want to use spade ends, then the Middlesex Angling Centre supply two excellent patterns, the Owner and the Kinryu. Many anglers will already be familiar with the Owner, but the Kinryu warrants special mention as it has features I have not seen on spade ends before. Firstly it has a small angled notch near the spade which should help prevent the knot slipping, and secondly, it has a small groove under the spade where your line should sit. Both hooks are in-turned point with a short shank and wide gape. If you order some, ask about sizes, because they go in the opposite way to the Redditch scale, and in both odd and even numbers. They come in good quality re-sealable plastic envelopes, which I like, and which contain instructions for tying the hooks on.

BENDS & GAPES

There are many different shapes of bend available, though in the main these concern the match angler far more than they do the carp angler, and I don't feel the need to go into any detail here. In most carp fishing applications, the standard and well tried round bend is adequate, and that is how many carp hooks are made.

The size of the gape, that is the distance between the point and the shank, may have some relevance to the carp angler in that it may determine whether the hook catches up in the carp's mouth. In theory, the wider the gape, the more likely it is to catch up. Also in theory, the wider the gape, the further out of line with the hook point is the pull, and the more likely is the hook to pull out; unless of course it has gone right through the carp's mouth and emerged on the other side, which is more likely to happen with a wide gape than a narrow one. The pressure will then be off the point, and the hook will be less likely to lose its hold. Bear in mind that theory may not be proved in practice; there are many unquantifiable variables in operation when a carp picks up your hook-bait, and theory and practice can be a long way apart.

STRAIGHT/REVERSED (offset)

A standard straight hook is one that has the point parallel to the shank in all planes. The reversed hook, or as it is sometimes known, the offset hook, is one that has the point at a different angle to the shank when viewed in such a way that the shank is furthest from you, and the point nearest to you. Once again, the advantages offered by each are arguable. The straight hook is probably better at pulling through soft baits such as paste, luncheon meat or bread. The reversed hook offers another angle of attack and may help when using the hair as an anti-eject mechanism.

IN-POINT/OUT-POINT/STRAIGHT POINT

Initially all hooks were designed with a straight point, and on balance I think one would be as well advised to use these as any other. There is nothing intrinsically wrong with straight points – but the in-turned and out-turned points may offer an advantage in some situations. The first deviation from the straight point was the in-turned, or beak, point. The first time I saw these in-turned points was on sea hooks. I'm not sure why they were originally designed, but this type of point has now found its way onto many of the hooks we use for freshwater fishing. Perhaps the most popular of these is the Au Lion D'Or, a hook which I have used extensively with great success. It is said of these hooks that once they are in, they rarely drop out, the in-turned point tending to bury the hook deeper, having less of a tearing action than straight or out-turned points. To some extent this may be true – I have fished waters where I have hardly lost a fish on the Au Lion D'Ors; but then, I have also fished waters where I have hardly landed a fish on them! There may be a disadvantage in using hooks with in-turned points in that the point may fail to make contact with the fish's mouth, and the carp may eject them more easily. For that reason, I think hooks with an in-turned point should always be offset, giving a better chance of them becoming caught up. One advantage of the in-turned point is that they may be less easily blunted by contact with gravel bars, or other hard objects.

Out-pointed hooks, as their name implies have the point slightly out, away from the shank. The thinking behind this is that they will easily gain an initial hold in the carp's mouth. Because of the angle of the point, it will be appreciated that if these hooks are only nicked in, then a heavy strike may easily pull them out, as they will tend to pull over. It may therefore be of advantage to gradually tighten on a take when using these hooks. They were primarily designed for use with the hair-rig, the out-turned point achieving that crucial initial prick.

If you are unsure as to how your favourite hook pattern will behave under pressure, why not buy a cod from your fishmonger and try them out. You'll learn a lot like that, and you'll have something for tea afterwards!

LONG POINT/SHORT POINT

A simple exercise in logic dictates that if a hook has a short point, then the taper leading to that point will be steep. On a long-pointed hook the taper will be shallow. On most hooks, lf not all, the barb is positioned at the fat end of the taper so that all of the point must penetrate before the barb becomes covered and therefore effective. With a short-pointed hook, the barb may not have so far to travel before it penetrates, but the relative steepness of the taper leading to the point may have a detrimental effect upon it doing so. On a hook with a long point, the barb will have further to travel before becoming embedded, but this will be facilitated by the shallow taper. It would seem to be a case of swings and roundabouts, and the best choice may lay somewhere between the two. In theory, the long point would be weaker, though I have never suffered from this problems, which I think would only really occur with exceptionally long points. On balance I would go for the longer point, which is also easier to sharpen, if you do sharpen your hooks. If you are using barbless hooks, then there surely is no choice – it must be the long needle-like point every time.

STRENGTH/FORGED/NON-FORGED

The strength of a fishing hook is largely dictated by the thickness of the wire used in its manufacture. Therefore, the stronger the hook, the heavier it will be, and this may in some cases affect your bait presentation. Additional strength can be given to a relatively fine wired hook by the process of forging the bend – slightly flattening the metal from the sides. I have read of some anglers doubting that this process does in fact work. I am no expert in metallurgy so my views are very much that of the layman, but the principle of flattening one side to gain strength in one plane does seem sound; to take an extreme example, imagine an ordinary 12 inch ruler. It will bend easily if you bend it one way, with the flat side up – but you try and bend it against the sharp side. It may be argued that strengthening in one plane will weaken in another; this may be so, but the forging process in a hook is not extreme, and gives additional strength in the plane where it is most needed. It almost goes without saying that hook strength should be related to line strength – it is of little point using strong hooks with line of a strength that won't enable you to take advantage of that hook; and equally, little use using line strong enough to open up the hook you are using.

SIZES

Related to strength is size. Obviously the bigger the hook the heavier, and in most cases, the stronger it is. Hook size is often related to bait size, and I will cover that in greater detail in the section on rigs (though you've probably read that already!). I have caught good carp on hooks as small as size 14, and as large as 2/0. If you think you need to go for a small hook, say a 10 or 12, then you obviously will need something reasonably strong. An excellent, and very strong small hook is the Drennan Super Specialist, a hook I have great faith in. These have a straight point, but lf you want a strong small hook with an in-turned point, try the Terry Eustace super strong hooks. Generally the most useful hook sizes are in the range of 2-8, on the Redditch scale.

SHARPNESS/SHARPENING TOOLS

As the process of chemical sharpening of hooks has been perfected, sharpening your own hooks has almost become a thing of the past. Almost all of the popular makes are now supplied with extremely sharp points, which is particularly important on the self-hooking rigs. If the hook point becomes blunt, it is probably better to replace it with a new hook. If you have a rig set up and a bait tied on, and for some reason have to retrieve your bait in the middle of the night, only to find the hook point has been slightly blunted by contact with a gravel bar, then you probably will sharpen it yourself, rather than re-tie the rig. I do anyway, and I find the best implement for doing so is a small saw-file. They are quite long, so I break mine in two, and keep one half in my carp box, and the other in my pike box. They put a superb point on a hook. On a carbon steel hook, sharpening will remove the protective coating, so you should look out for signs of rust.

There may be a possibility of an extremely sharp hook point digging into a bony part of a fish's mouth, whereas a less sharp hook would slide off the bone and find a hold in the flesh. If a hold in bone is obtained, it will obviously be a very tenuous one, and may result in a lost fish. On occasions I have lost carp and have found the very tip of the hook-point to be bent over. The reason for this could be that the hook has dug into the bone and failed to find a hold in the flesh.

Although I mostly use chemically sharpened hooks now, I am still a little wary of the above happening, though time has proved the exceedingly sharp hook in general to be at least as effective as the very sharp hook.

LENGTH OF SHANK

Most carp hooks have a shank of medium length. There was a belief that long-shanked hooks applied more leverage on the hook-hold, and were therefore more likely to result in lost fish. I think that theory has been shot down in flames by the success of the bent hook rig. However, apart from the principle behind the bent hook, I can see no real reason for using long-shanked hooks, except perhaps that, even in standard un-bent form, they do have an angle of pull more in line with the point than the standard shank length. Personally when not using the bent hook, I prefer to use hooks with a medium length shank. I think you would be hard put to do anything else anyway, as apart from the bent hooks, I don't think anyone markets a long-shank hook especially for carp fishing.

BARBED/MICRO-BARBED/ BARBLESS/OUT-BARBED

The barbed/barbless choice, except where rules dictate, is very much a personal thing, and I know anglers who swear by both types. The days of those large, rank barbs seem to have passed, and when we talk about barbs these days, we are talking usually about small neat barbs, or micro barbs. These are what I use; I spend much of my carp fishing time on waters where takes are not that frequent – I don't use barbless hooks because I am afraid they may fall out. It may be alright to lose the occasional fish due to fishing a barbless hook – but when you only get one take a year…!

Barbless hooks do have an advantage in that they probably go in easier, having no barb to impede penetration. I can't help having the feeling though that they also may come out easier. I know if you are keeping a tight line on a fish, that shouldn't happen; and that if you are fishing snag and weed-free waters, you should always be able to keep a tight line: but, as I said, when you only get one take a year! It has been argued that barbless hooks do less damage to the fish. However, I think there would be very little difference between the damage done by a barbless hook, and that done by one with a micro-barb, so long as care is taken in the removal. If the hook won't come out easily, either cut the point off, or cut the line and pull it through the other way. The eye could be cut off to facilitate this. If you do use barbless hooks, and make them so by crushing the barb, remember this may damage the surface coating, leaving a spot prone to rusting near the weakest point of the hook.

Out-barbed hooks have only just found their way onto the market. So far as I know, they were first mentioned by George Sharman in his excellent book "Carp and the Carp Angler", a book that did much to revive my interest in carp fishing. At the time George was going to great lengths to make his own out-barbed hooks, and he goes into some detail as to why he believes them effective. Though the theory of having the barb follow the point, rather than preceding it seems sound, the effort of producing such hooks was beyond me, and I have never tried them. One should consider that a barb in this position is more likely to suffer damage than a standard one. For anyone who is interested, outbarb hooks are now marketed by Partridge, under the name of 'Kevin Maddocks. Outbarb Specimen Hooks'.

CORROSION RESISTANCE

This is perhaps a non starter these days, as I suspect most anglers have tied on a new hook long before their old one is showing any serious signs of corrosion. I have noticed though that many of the chemically sharpened hooks begin to show signs of corrosion after a very short time. This is not serious though, and can be scraped off with your thumbnail; anathema I know to those who recommend every single hook showing the slightest blemish should be discarded! But as some hooks show signs of discolouration after only 12 hours in water, I doubt there has been any loss in strength in that time. It may be a dangerous thing to say, but I have often fished with hooks with small blemishes on them, and have yet to have one let me down.

Apart from the normal lacquering of the hook to prevent corrosion, one company, Partridge of Redditch, produces a range of hooks called the Grey Shadow, which are coated with 'Niflor', a coating which combines the corrosion resistance of nickel phosphorous with the special qualities of PTFE. Partridge have put considerable research into this product, and have come up with a coating with two definite advantages; corrosion and wear resistance. I think this will be of more interest to the fly fisherman who, having tied a complicated dressing, wants the hook to last for some time. I suspect most carp anglers renew their hooks frequently, but for the lazy ones among you, Niflor may have something to offer. Partridge use this coating on several of their extensive range of carp hooks, so you may find your favourite pattern is produced with this coating. The Grey Shadow range includes the Rod Hutchinson WW's, Jack Hilton's and the Maddocks Cassien hooks. Niflor reduces friction, which should aid penetration. However, considering the very short distance the hook has to move before the fish is hooked, I have to reserve judgement on whether a 'Niflor' coating is going to make a vast difference to the number of fish caught. Unless your results improved dramatically I think it would be very difficult indeed to evaluate such a product in this respect. However, if you aren't catching, anything new is worth a try.

COLOUR

Here's an interesting one that doesn't seem to have reared its head in a while. Most hooks are either brown, or a trendy black, though the Partridge Niflor coating already mentioned gives a nice subdued grey colour. When it was thought that carp would be put off by the sight of hooks, they were made to look as inconspicuous as possible. Why then there are so many black hooks – one of the most conspicuous colours, which I think hardly exists in nature. I don't know. I have seen some green ones, but they were not of a good pattern and never caught on. (pun not intended!) Gold ones with sweet-corn, I presume to fool carp into thinking the hook was a strangely shaped piece of corn; come on now! Stainless steel hooks, coloured silver, have also had their day. Apart from the fact that the hooks manufactured in this material were a superb pattern, some anglers believe that the little silver glint may well attract a curious carp to their bait. That may have been the case – you would have trouble proving otherwise! All things being equal, I think the fairly standard bronze colour is good enough, though I honestly don't think hook colour, particularly with bottom baits on a hair, makes any difference at all – though it might be interesting to try hooks in silly colours such as fluorescent orange and yellow!

BENT HOOKS

I don't know who first discovered, or re-discovered the bent hook. I think it had its origins somewhere around Longfield, and has been credited to someone known only to me as 'Secret John'. Well done John – it's brilliant! I said at the start, re-discovered. I say this because I have seen hooks of a similar pattern in the Mustad display cabinet, dating from many, many years ago. I suspect that the significance of having the eye in line with the point had been realised then, but I'm sure the concept of the hook flipping round as it is drawn across the fish's lips is original. Most anglers using this hook were originally bending long-shanked fly hooks with pliers. There are several 'ready-bent' versions available now, and I have seen some bent into some weird and wonderful shapes. The point at where the hook is bent is said to be absolutely critical. As long as you bend it about one third of the way down from the eye, I don't think being 25 thou out will make much difference. The hook is bent until the point is pointing at the bottom of the eye, which should ideally be a down-turned eye. This gives an angle of pull directly in line with the point, making it unlikely that the hook will pull out.

The bent hook is usually used in sizes from 4 to 8. I have found with some patterns, once you go smaller than a standard size 6, the hook doesn't perform

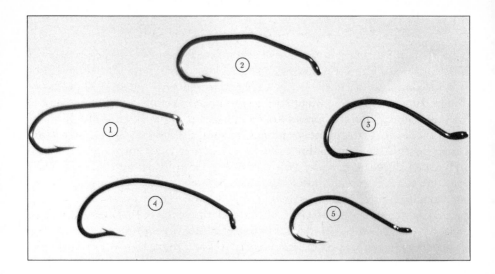

1. Bent Drennan Lure Hook (6)
2. Gardner Bent Hook (6)
3. Partridge WS Specimen Hunter (Simpsons Carpcatcher) (6)
4. Partridge Piggy Back (4)
5. Drennan Starpoint (4)

the function of flipping over as well as in the larger sizes. The length of the shank would seem to be the important factor here. There are those who recommend all bent hooks should be barbless, as due to the angle of pull, they tend to be difficult to get out. This may be so, but up to now I have had no problems. If you do, then consider going barbless.

Two excellent patterns for making your own bent hooks are the Kamasan lure hook, and the Drennan lure hooks which don't seem to break in the pliers as easily as they did a year ago! Please bear in mind that a hook which you have bent yourself is unlikely to be as strong as one which has been bent at the factory.

Various shops will sell you ready bent lure hooks, and Gardner do their own, a very strong hook made by Sprite – a name that will already be familiar to many carp anglers. These come in sizes 6 and 8. Although, the 8 appears to be bent in the wrong place, Richard Gardner tells me that results when using it are very good.

Other specialised hooks...

DRENNAN STARPOINT

The Starpoint hooks manufactured by Drennan are a follow on from the bent hook concept which has already been discussed. What is radically different about them is that the point, instead of being round in section, is shaped like a four pointed star. This in theory will give easier penetration, while the shape of the hook should ensure that, due to the angle of pull, once in it stays in. They come barbed and barbless, and the 'splayed' shape of the point may help barbless hooks of this pattern to stay in better than a more conventional barbless hook. They do not flip round so reliably as the longer shanked 'bent hook' and have not been readily available for long enough for me to evaluate them properly. The reviews that have been published have been very favourable. I have been using them, but it is far too early to form an opinion. So far I have hooked one fish on them – a big one – and it came off...

PARTRIDGE KARPERHAAK AND PIGGYBACK HOOKS

Partridge's Karperhaak is a similarly shaped hook to the Drennan Starpoint, but with a normal point, and longer shank. They are very popular in Holland and Belgium and are marketed in the U.K. by Simpsons of Turnford under the name 'Simpson Carpcatcher hooks'. They flip round like the bent hook in sizes 6 upwards, and come barbed and barbless. The barbless version features Partridge's 'Arrowpoint' which is slightly splayed to help it stay in.

Partridge's main contribution to the bent hooks are the Piggyback hooks. I'd be a bit embarrassed going into a tackle shop asking for them, but they certainly function well, differing from do-it-yourself bent hooks in that instead of a sharp bend, they have a steady curve and a slightly out-turned hook point. The eye is down-turned, they are chemically sharpened, black in colour, and very strong. This extra strength could give you an advantage over bent hooks made from normal lure hooks, which although performing quite well against big fish in open water, are a little unsafe to use near snags. I know some anglers who have had bent lure hooks break in that situation, something that hooks which are actually bent during the manufacturing process are not likely to do. They are available in sizes 4, 6 and 8. The smaller size is of particular interest, as the normal lure hook is not strong enough to use in a size 8, and unlike many other bent size 8's, this one does actually flip round and dig in.

John Miles admires an upper double taken on a side hooked particle set-up.

KNOTS

Is there anything so personal to an angler as the knot he uses to tie his hook on? That vital connection between man and monster! When most anglers were using monofilament hook-links, probably the majority of them used the five-turn blood knot to tie on eyed hooks. In my early days as an angler, this was the only knot I knew, let alone used; and I used it un-tucked. How I got away with that I'll never know – I can't tie an un-tucked blood knot that doesn't slip now! With the use of braided lines it was soon discovered that another knot may be needed to avoid breakage caused by strangulation of the line. One of the first anglers to realise this, to his cost, was Fred Buller; if he had known it sooner, the pike record may be considerably higher than it is now; out of reach even! (see 'Pike' by Fred Buller).

The first knot I know of that was used to overcome this problem was the 'Bimini twist', and some anglers have gone to the lengths of soaking the end of their hook-links in polyurethane varnish, then letting it dry before tying it to hook or swivel. The 'Bimini twist' is one hell of a knot to tie, and I'd hate to have to attempt it in the dark, or with cold hands! Rather than try to describe a knot that probably relatively few of you will even attempt to tie, can I refer you to Jim Gibbinson's excellent book 'Big Water Carp' which contains comprehensive instructions? There is also a description in Fred Buller's 'Pike'. Latterly, anglers use knots that require the line to be taken though the eye twice, thus avoiding strangulation by taking the pressure off the knot. This coupled with the fact that braided hook-links are generally used in slightly heavier breaking strains than are actually required has largely overcome the problem of strangulation. Knots though are a very individual thing, and most anglers will stick to their tried and trusted tyings. I too have my favourites, and once again I will tempt providence and say they have never let me down. The only knot I use, for tying on hooks, swivels and shock leaders, is the Grinner, in one form or another. For tying on monofilament line, I use the standard four turn Grinner knot, with one turn through the eye. For all dacrons, and the Kryston Silkworm and Merlin, I use the same knot, but only use two turns. For Kryston multi-strand and supersilk I use a five turn Grinner, with two turns through the eye. For joining mainline or leader to the swivel, I use a four or five turn Grinner with one turn through the eye. For joining leaders to main line, I use a double Grinner, usually making three turns with the thicker line, and four turns with the thinner. You will note that I do not place emphasis on taking two turns through the eye of the hook. This system was first brought to my attention by George Sharman, when in his book he described the two-turn slip knot for use with braided hook-links. The

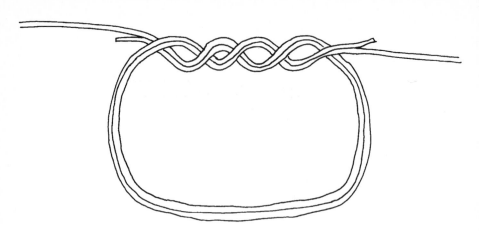

Double overhand or four-turn water knot.

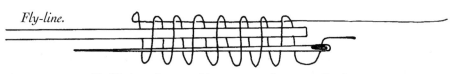

Fly-line.

Needle knot for attaching mono or dacron to fly-line.

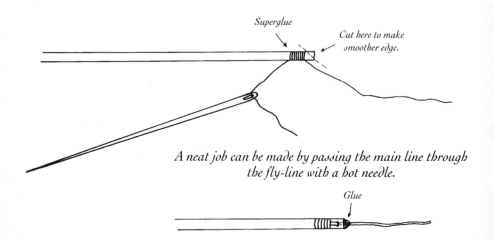

Superglue

Cut here to make smoother edge.

A neat job can be made by passing the main line through the fly-line with a hot needle.

Glue

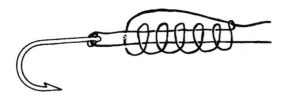

Twice through the eye Clinch Knot.

Knots for joining 2 lengths of line

The Barrel Knot, looking suspiciously like the double grinner.
From a book published in the early 1940's.

The double grinner — experiment with the number of turns.

principle is that the two turns through the eye take the pressure off the actual knot, and that only a very basic knot is then needed. I have used the two-turn slip-knot but could never achieve the sort of knot strengths George did. Neither could I see the advantage in using two turns through the hook eye when using such a superb knot as the Grinner. It seemed critical that the two turns did not cross one another, and in practice, when tightening up the knot, this often happened. Even if it doesn't happen at that stage, you will more often than not find it has happened while a fish was being played. I have tested the two-turn Grinner with one turn through the eye against the same knot with two turns through the eye. The differences were marginal, and came out in favour of the one-turn version as often as the two-turn. Strangulation does not occur simply because there are only two turns of the knot around the hook link. If there were five or six, then under pressure there may be a problem. I use the two turn through the eye version when using Kryston multi-strand and Supersilk simply because these materials are quite slippery, and the two turns seem to be necessary to prevent slippage under pressure. For that reason, the four or five turn Grinner is also used with these materials. You will find the multi-strands easier to knot if you wet them first; this helps to ensure all the strands are taken up evenly, which is essential for a strong knot.

I know some anglers who tie the five turn grinner with the line doubled over, though I haven't found this necessary myself.

As I have said, knots are a personal choice, and I have friends who are still using the tucked blood knot with all the new hook-link materials, and have no complaints. There are many others, such as the Clinch knot, the Turle and the Palomar. I wouldn't tell you which knot to use, but if you asked for a recommendation, I would say that the Grinner, in one form or another, will cover most of your needs. It also has the added advantage of being easy to tie; indeed, once you are familiar with it, it can easily be tied with your eyes shut.

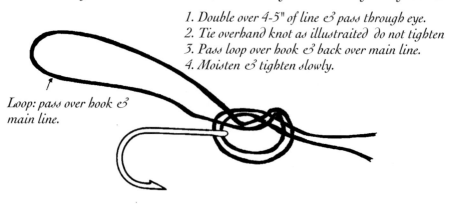

1. Double over 4-5" of line & pass through eye.
2. Tie overhand knot as illustraited do not tighten
3. Pass loop over hook & back over main line.
4. Moisten & tighten slowly.

Loop: pass over hook & main line.

Palomar Knot.

24

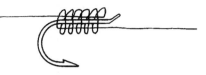
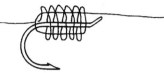

Knots for spade ends.

1. Multi-turned whipping knot.   *2. Domhoff knot.*

These knots can also be used for tying stop knots.

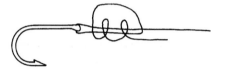
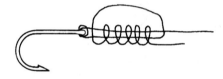

Two turn Grinner   *Twice through the eye, five turn grinner.*

*Grinners: tighten gently by pulling short end of line,
when knot is closed, moisten line and fully
tighten by pulling other end of line.*

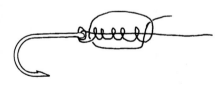
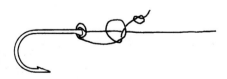

Two turn tucked blood knot.   *Two turn slip knot.*

For additional security, some anglers superglue their knots, particularly with multi-strands, and you can do this if you wish.

For those of you using spade ends, there is far less choice of knots to use. The only knots I know of for tying spade ends are the Domhoff, and the multi-whipping knot, both of which are illustrated.

One thing I should mention here is that many people believe that the only indication of knot failure is when line goes right at the knot. If it goes anywhere else, they blame the hook-link. With some of the latest hook-link materials, knot failure can be indicated by a breakage up to several inches from the knot, so if you get a break an inch from the hook, think carefully about the knot you are using.

Gary Bond with a side hooked 19lb capture.

HOOKLINKS

Like most other items of carp tackle as we move into the nineties, the choice of hook-link materials seem endless. Even when you have decided which one you want to use, there is still the critical question of length to consider. In this section I'll describe all the hook-links I know of, describing both their advantages and disadvantages.

MONOFILAMENT

The original hook-link material, still used by many anglers, some famous ones, who are still not convinced alternative materials offer any great advantage. Monofilament lines have improved tremendously over the past 10 years or so, becoming more reliable, thinner for a given breaking strain, and more supple. If you want to use monofilament hook-links, then you can of course use a piece of whatever main line you are using, and in some applications, this would probably suffice. Far better though would be to look at some of the new, fine diameter lines such as Drennan double-strength, Platil Soft or my own favourite, Trilene. Drennan double-strength suffered a fair amount of criticism when anglers started using it as a main line. I myself lost a carp when the line broke in a situation where it should not have done so. Things have settled down since then, and while some anglers seem able to use it successfully as a main line, it is generally accepted that its best application is as a hook-link. As far as I know, it is the finest line around for its breaking strain, at least in strengths of practical use for carp fishing. Platil Soft is another excellent line, and though I have only used it for barbel fishing, I can see it could be used effectively in a hook-link for carp. Trilene XL I have used for 7 or 8 years, as a main line, and, occasionally, as a hook-link. It is a superb line in all respects, reliable, fine, supple and discreet. It has never let me down, and I don't know what more anyone could ask for in a fishing line. In 6, 8 or 10lb breaking strains, it makes a very good hook-link material. Not biassed, am I!

One of the latest developments in fine diameter lines is D.A.M. Tectan. Mostly it is only available in low breaking strains. I know you can buy it in 6 or 8lbs b.s., and am told that it is made in heavier breaking strains. I have not used it, but have a friend who has, though only for chub. He recommends it, so it may be worth looking at.

There was a short period when anglers were fishing with very fine monofilament hook-links, using a length of power gum as a shock absorber. I used to do this years ago when fly fishing for trout, when I had to use flies so small they could only be properly presented on very fine leaders; indeed, it was for this purpose that power gum was first invented. I don't think it is a good idea to fish for big carp in this way, as even if you land them, it will probably take an awfully long time, and tire the fish unnecessarily. It didn't matter much to the trout as they invariably got banged on the head anyway!

DACRONS AND BRAIDED NYLONS

Dacron was originally a trade name, but as it has now become a noun used to describe many of the braided hook-links: I shall continue to use the word dacron to refer to them collectively. I think there are now almost as many 'carp' dacrons on the market as there are hook patterns! I am therefore going to have to generalise somewhat, only going into detail on the ones I have found best. These lines were first used as hook-links because their suppleness allowed baits to act more naturally in the water. Mostly they are black, and have a relatively poor knot strength, so that their use in 12 and 15lb breaking strains became the norm even when fishing main lines of 6-10 lbs. It is also said of them that they do not stretch and therefore assist in hooking a fish; I don't know who is kidding whom here, but virtually all the dacrons I have tried stretch like very fine tape. This enables them to flex more easily. The tightness of weave of the individual fibres making up the braid also has some influence on suppleness; the looser the weave, the more supple the dacron seems to be. Some have a waxy coating on them; I'm not sure what advantage this is supposed to offer, but it does make the material stiffer. One of the bets of the older dacrons was undoubtedly Black Spider by Milwards, and some of the original material from Ryobi was also good. I used these a lot, and caught quite a few good fish on them. More recently, I have found the Garcia dacron to be far superior to any other line of this type, being very supple and smooth; and this one doesn't stretch. I have used it successfully in breaking strains as high as 20lbs. Its only drawback is that it is black. That may not matter, but when everyone else was using black dacron, I sometimes felt I wanted to use another colour. I have contacted the manufacturers to see if they could make it in any other colours, but apparently they cannot. That is a pity.

A relatively new dacron that is available in alternative colours is made by Drennan. It comes in two colours, a weedy green, and a beige. In the 12lb breaking strain it is extremely supple, and has relatively good knot strength. I feel the 15lb b.s. is a little stiff, but in most cases would be happy to use the 12lbs. One thing to remember when using dacron is that it does absorb water, making it heavier, and though I don't think this ever caused me any great problems, it is possible it could affect a finally balanced presentation.

I have only used one braided nylon, and that is made by Cortland, the American firm who are famous for their excellent fly-lines. This line is interesting in that it is dyed with alternating colours, green, brown, sand and grey, each segment of colour measuring about 9 inches. You can therefore trim off a piece that matches the colour of the lake bed you are fishing over. I like the idea, but, unfortunately, I find the 15lb b.s. rather stiff, and the 10lb having insufficient knot-strength for me to risk it when fishing for big carp.

Gary Bond with a big double caught on a paste bait with the hook embedded in it. (1979).

DENTAL FLOSS

Dental floss was one of the forerunners to the multi-strands and the latest very supple braids. I haven't used it much, as I discovered an excellent multi-strand about the same time as anglers began using dental floss. Dental floss comes waxed, or unwaxed, and the unwaxed version seems to be the more supple. Some makes are better than others, but to me, none of them seemed strong enough to risk when fishing for very big carp on waters where takes were infrequent. If you want to try dental floss, then I suggest you buy several different makes, and test them thoroughly before using them. It does make a very supple hook-link, is cheap, and can be dyed any colour, or combination of colours you wish. You can of course use it doubled up, which virtually doubles the breaking strain with little significant increase in stiffness.

KRYSTON

As anyone who has read the Carp Society's book, *For the Love of Carp* will know, I have been messing around with alternative hook-link materials for many years now, mainly in order to find something that was supple, low diameter, and not black! Multi-strands are terrific, but have their problems, as most of you will by now have found out. I was delighted when Kryston brought out their Silkworm, and used it almost exclusively, landing some good carp with no problems at all. I know there were teething troubles with some of the original materials, but am glad to see they have now been sorted out, and the four hook-link materials now being marketed are all superb.

The multi-strand, as many of you will know, is exactly what it says - a hook-link made from many very fine strands loosely held together, and which separate when in water, becoming virtually undetectable. The first mention I saw in print of a multi-stranded hook-link was in the BCSG magazine, the *Carp*. These hook-links were made by glueing ten pieces of one pound line (or was it twenty pieces of half pound line - no matter) together at either end of the hook-link, giving an overall breaking strain of 10lbs, but with only the stiffness of one of the strands of line. These did work, but were fiddly to set up, each strand having to be of exactly the same length. And they would cut through easily too, which frightened the life out of me! The later multi-strands are made from much finer fibres, though each one has a surprising strength for its diameter. Because there are so many of them, and because they are made of a material which is highly resistant to abrasion, they are both reliable, and effective in use. There have been tangling problems associated with these hook-links, though there is now a product designed to facilitate their use, which I will come to later.

For anyone interested in reading more detail on multi-strands, I would refer you to my chapter on that subject in *For the Love of Carp*. If you haven't already got a copy, then go and buy one - it's a good read, and you'll be helping to support Redmire. The other three materials, Silkworm, Merlin and Supersilk, are all braids, and all different. Silkworm and Merlin appear basically to be Kryston multi-strand, woven together with thread of differing colours, preventing the strands from parting. All have excellent abrasion resistance; in fact it can be a right bastard trying to cut them! Silkworm is a very low diameter, and exceptionally supple braid, which is coloured brown and white, and when wet looks an inconspicuous brown colour. I believe next year's Silkworm will be coloured brown, green and white, camouflaging it even further, and that it has also been altered slightly to make it even more supple. It has been specifically weighted to be just below neutral buoyancy, to facilitate fishing over weed, or very soft silt, and for use with finely balanced baits.

Merlin is a similar braid to Silkworm, and has similar properties, but is slightly thicker than Silkworm for a given breaking strain, though this shouldn't worry you. The wet knot strength of these products seems, if anything, to be understated and I would be quite happy to use the Merlin in 12lbs b.s. Merlin is coloured green and white, looking a drab green when wet. It is weighted with heavier denier polyester than Silkworm, so should lay flat on the bottom in those circumstances where you feel this to be necessary.

I used to find when using various multi-stranded materials, that it was important to renew the hook-link frequently. This is definitely not necessary with Silkworm or Merlin, and it will delight lazy anglers to know that they can be used almost indefinitely. Perhaps I shouldn't have said that - I don't suppose Kryston want you all using the same piece of hook-link all season!

Supersilk was, I believe, formerly marketed by Lee Jackson under the name of "Python" (what is it with all these snakes!). This is an ultra-fine braid, extremely supple, especially when wet. It is exceptionally strong for its diameter, and is coloured white. If this bothers you, it can easily be dyed using a felt tip marker, preferably the water-proof ones used by fly-tiers to colour feathers, or by soaking in luke warm dylon (don't boil it!), though it soon colours up when in use. Again, just above neutral buoyancy. I like this one very much, though experience has shown that you will have to be a little more fussy about knots when using it. There is a small booklet enclosed with all of these products, informing anglers how to get the best out of them. I have tested all the lines in the Kryston range, both wet and dry, using the knots I described earlier, and found that with the exception of one of them, they all broke either at, or above their stated wet knot strength. The only one that didn't was the 15lb Silkworm, which occasionally broke at 14lbs. I'm not going to worry too much about that!

Silkworm comes in 4lb, 8lb, 10lb, 12lb, 15lb and 25lb; Merlin in 8lb, 10lb,

Above: John Read returning a mirror of 22.14 caught on a hair rigged boilie.
Below: Gary Bond cradles a lovely 27lb mirror trapped by the Alec Wellend rig.

12lb and 15lb; and Supersilk in 14lb. These are the wet knot strengths when using the knots recommended by Kryston (usually the 5 turn Grinner with 2 turns through the hook eye). When we were all using dacron or braided nylon, mostly you had to use 15lbs b.s. to obtain a knot strength of 10/11lbs. This is not so with the Kryston materials, and in most general fishing situations, you could comfortably use the 12lbs b.s.

GAMASTRAND/GAMABRAID

These are Kevin Nash's contribution to the latest generation of supple hook-links. Gamastrand is a multi-strand, similar in appearance to Kryston's, and comes in 10lb, 25lb and 50lb breaking strains. Gamabraid is a braided version of the multi-strand, available in 6lb, 8lb, 10lb, 12lb, 15lb and 25lb breaking strains. I haven't used them for fishing with, though not through any personal preference for anything else. I started out with the Krystons, and finding them good enough see no need to change. Kevin Nash would, I am sure, tell me I don't know what I have been missing! Whatever, I don't intend running a technical comparison against Kryston, and much of what I have said about the Kryston braids could probably be said about the Gamabraids. I don't know (or care!) whether they are made of the same materials, but I do know that the 'Gamas' have their devotees, and that, like Kryston, many big fish are caught on them. All I have done is to test them at home, and have found them to be very fine and supple. There is no recommended knot supplied, so to test the breaking strains I tried several, and found the 5 turn Grinner taken twice through the eye to be best. Using this knot with the braids, I achieved a consistent breaking strain slightly above that stated by the manufacturer. I could find little difference between the 10lb and 12lb breaking strain. Gamabraid is coloured green and white, and seems to be around neutral buoyancy. When testing the multi-strand, which like the Kryston is coloured white, for once I found the Grinner wanting. One has to be so careful with knots when using multi-strands, and you must ensure the strands do not get misaligned in the tying. The best knot for Gamastrand appears to be the Palomar, which is illustrated in the knots section.

OTHER BRAIDS

Drennan are now marketing two braids which are similar to the Silkworm and Merlin. I haven't used them, but tests show the breaking to be consistently understated, which is probably why they seem quite stiff. The only other similar braid I have seen is marketed by Barker International, under the name of Microply. I don't know much about this firm, and have neither tried 'nor tested this braid. If you want to investigate it, it is quite simple, coloured black and white, and available in 10lbs, 15lbs and 25lbs breaking strain.

OTHER MULTI-STRANDS

As I mentioned earlier, I have used multi-stranded materials other than Kryston, indeed was using them as early as 1982, when Kryston was but a twinkle in Dave Chilton's eye! There are alternative sources, and some are excellent, though do require the hook-link to be changed frequently; and none of them have the abrasion resistance of Kryston, though some of them are more supple. To give you some ideas you can use dapping flosses (though the best ones aren't made any more), bow-strings (archer's), and bits pulled from terylene rope. You will need to change them frequently, as they seem to lose strength after they have dried out.

Alan returning a 23lb leather caught on a top hooked boilie.

LEADS

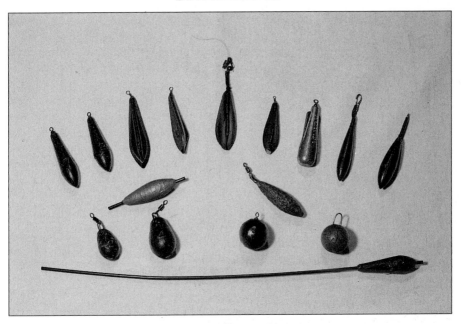

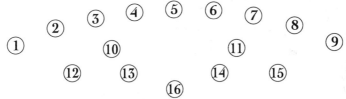

(1) Standard Carp Bamb (2¼oz) (9) Garden Tailed Bomb
(2) Standard Carp Bomb (2½oz) (10) Zipp In-line Lead (affix tubing)
(3) Tri Lobe 2oz (11) Zipp Lead (standard)
(4) Tri Lobe 1½ oz (12) Nash Bolt Lead
(5) Early Nash Cruise Lead (13) Nash Bolt Lead
(6) Gardener Riser (14) Garden Round Lead
(7) Eustace Butt Bomb (15) Hounslow Angling Centre
(8) Garden Stelth Lead Round Lead
Showing Attatchment (16) Anti-Tangle Tubing and Lead.

The main thing that has happened to a carp angler's leads in the last 20 years is that they have got bigger and bigger.

Starting from the point where any lead on the line was anathema we have now reached the stage where anglers are using leads as heavy as 6 ounces for carp fishing. The heaviest lead I have used for carp fishing is 3oz, and the only time I have used anything heavier is when I have been fishing from a boat in the sea. Using leads of a pound and upwards detracted greatly from the pleasure of playing the fish. I don't know how a double figure carp would feel being played through a 6oz lead; I have a feeling I'll never find out! As well as changes in size, the other main change, if we ignore the fact that weights of 1oz and under are not actually being made of lead any longer, is the different shapes that are now available. While most leads today largely conform to the basic shape of the Arlesey bomb, designed in the 1950's by the late Richard Walker, there have been one or two attempts to, so to speak, break out of that mould, to achieve a specific purpose. In the main, efforts have been centred around increasing casting distance.

One of the best examples of this is the streamlined Zipp lead. I have used these, and they do cast very well, though I have found the increase in distance attained to be slight. They come with a swivel already attached; I don't particularly like this idea, as if you then attach them to your line by a link, or snap swivel, the flexible joint obtained is quite long, and difficult to cover efficiently with tubing, and the hook-link can quite easily become caught around it.

I believe Tri-lobe were the first people to bring out a fluted lead. What their original purpose was, I don't know, though I do remember reading that they were supposed to increase casting distance. I am unable to agree with this, but what they do superbly whether by intention, or design, is to rise quickly in the water when you lift the rod to reel in. This is invaluable when fishing over snags, or in silt which may contain mussels. I can say from experience that they work very well in the latter case, even a 2oz lead coming up very quickly, and not sinking too deeply into the silt in the first place. There have been copies made of this type of lead, I believe called the 'riser'. Though I have not used them myself, I assume they would perform a similar function. The very latest in leads that lift up in this way is the 'Buzz Bomb'. This is basically an Arlesey bomb with fins. It looks quaint, but it don't half work well! And it doesn't scutter about on the surface as much as the Tri-lobe. As far as I know, Terry Eustace is the only supplier of these at the moment. One other advantage with leads of this type is that if you are trying to position your bait on a slope, such as the side of a bar, they won't roll down to the bottom.

Another lead which has been around for some time is the one shaped basically like an Arlesey bomb, but with the bottom hollowed out to allow you to put your hookbait there. To fasten the hookbait in position I would advise that you drill two small holes crossways through the lead, and at right angles to each other, close to the bottom. You can then pass P.V.A. through these holes and make a small cradle which will hold the bait. The other alternative is to use Kryston no-tangle to glue the bait in, though this will take about 5 minutes to set, and won't work with oily baits. When set up properly, these leads cast miles! They can be a bit hard on hook baits though. I have retrieved bombs that have actually been bent after being cast to gravel bars just 6 feet below the surface. In this case, a bait affixed to the bottom of the lead may take a bit of a bashing! If you are fishing over silt, be aware that the lead will bury the bait, and ensure you pull back when you judge the P.V.A. to have melted. You can get P.V.A. which melts instantly on contact with water, and this would be the best to use in this case.

Two recent products are the round leads, and the 'Stealth' lead. These are completely opposite; the round leads being spherical, and the 'Stealth' leads being long and narrow. They have both been designed with an object in mind.

The round leads are an attempt to further improve the efficiency of the fixed lead set-up. With standard shape bombs, depending on which angle the fish picks up the bait, and the nature of the lake bottom (it won't happen if the lead is struck fast in silt!) the lead may have to be pulled around a short distance as it pivots about its base, before its full weight comes into effect. This small amount of movement can be enough to stop a wary carp in its tracks, and cause it to drop the bait before the hook is set. With round leads this movement is far more limited, and the full weight of the lead is apparent almost as soon as the hook-link is tightened. I can't really fault the theory of this, though in practice it is hard sometimes to know if you would have caught a fish anyway. On waters where the carp have seen everything, trying anything different is worthwhile, and the theory of the round lead certainly makes sense. They cast fairly well, though obviously the 6-ouncers won't go far unless you use a beach-caster! They do, however, made one hell of a splash!

They are available with either a metal loop or swivel to attach them to the line via a link swivel, or spigotted so the line can pass through the centre. The spigots protrude at either end, allowing you to push anti-tangle tubing over them. If I had to choose, I think I would prefer the ones which have a swivel to attach the line, as the metal loops are often too long and may allow the lead to roll before its weight is felt. This may also happen with the spigotted version.

The 'Stealth' leads are completely the opposite. Being long and thin, they cause a minimum of disturbance when they enter the water. This could well be useful when casting to a moving fish, though I do sometimes wonder whether the high frequency vibrations set up by a lead hitting the water do worry the fish that much. Mind you, I'm not sure whether I'd cast a 6oz round

John Miles with an upper twenty caught on a hair rigged particle.

lead to a spooky fish!

Owing to the shape of the 'Stealth' leads, they are obviously not going to perform as efficiently as a round lead in a fixed lead set-up. They do however give you a choice, and if you feel your carp are liable to leave the swim for the rest of the day if you cast a normal, or round lead to them, try the 'Stealth' leads.

I would think the size of water, and number of fish in it would be a consideration here. To illustrate, let me give some extreme examples: If your water is one acre, rich, with many feeding areas and contains few carp, and you cast a six ounce lead near some of them, they may leave that area for some time. Even fish 50 yards away may detect the disturbance, and if they are spooky fish, it may even put them off feeding for a while. They will not however, in a small water, be able to get that far from you, and if you have time to wait, they'll come back eventually.

If, on the other hand, your water is of 20 acres and fairly heavily stocked, then you are hardly likely to frighten all the fish, or even most of them. The one's that were too far away to be alarmed by the cast may well come over the baits later in the day. If you are on a 500 acre water with one fish in it, and you are fortunate to find it quietly feeding in a corner of the lake, then I wouldn't recommend you cast a 6oz round lead on his nose! I don't have to say why, do I?

One of the first suppliers of round leads was Ritchie MacDonald at the Hounslow Angling Centre. You can still get them from him, and you can get both round and Stealth leads from Gardner tackle. I like the Gardner round leads as they have a swivel to attach the line, rather than the longish wire loop. The swivel is set well into the lead allowing you to attach it close to the line for optimum effect. Their Stealth leads feature a quick change eye, removing the need to use a snap link. Don't, however, be tempted to fix it to the hook-link swivel - use something like the Drennan swivel bead, or push a Berkeley swivel onto your tubing.

Similar in concept to the round leads are the Kevin Nash bolt leads. These are short dumpy bombs designed to help increase the shock effect on the carp. They come in various sizes and though I haven't used them, I'm sure they would perform much the same function as the round lead.

Another fairly recent development is the 'in-line' or comet type lead. These leads are still basically shaped like the Arlesey bomb, but with a long length of anti-tangle tubing passed through them lengthways. The line is then passed through the tubing, giving a streamlined and relatively tangle-free set-up. Some of them have little wire loops fixed to the tubing to which you can PVA your bait to stop it flapping about during the cast. These do work well, and at one time it seemed everyone was using them. Lately, and for what reason I know not, most carp anglers I have seen have reverted to the standard leads, either with or without anti-tangle tube. One of the drawbacks I found with the comet type leads was that with most of them, it necessitated you carrying fairly long lengths of stiff tubing around. In the tackle bag, this invariably became bent, and this in turn would severely affect the casting range of this set up. Zipp introduced a flexible tube system, but for whatever reason, I don't see many anglers using it these days. I do have more to say on the actual tubing, but that is a topic in itself, and will be covered separately.

Kevin Nash did introduce a system of 'Cruise' leads, which were quite adaptable in that you could use them either as a standard lead, or an in-line lead. The concept was quite clever, meaning you no longer had to carry around a vast array of leads. Once again though, I don't see many anglers using them these days, and am not sure if they are still made.

Other leads that have been around for some time are the bullet lead, of which the spigotted round lead is more or less a larger version, and the coffin lead, which as its name suggests, is shaped like a coffin, the line passing through its centre. These leads are not much used by anglers these days, but in their larger sizes did have a brief revival in the early bolt rigs.

One last thing on leads. I will at various points in the text mention back-leads, and though these are not exactly a part of the rig, in case some anglers have not come across them, I had better explain what they are. In some situations, you may find it advantageous to fish with your main line tight to the bottom. Back leads are generally quite small, detachable weights which, after casting, can be slid down the line to rest on the bottom just under the rod-top. They are free running, and will slide down to the main lead when you reel in. Gardner tackle make a range of sizes which come with neat plastic clips to which you attach the leads yourself, or you can make your own.

LEAD COATINGS

It was a surprisingly long time ago now that anglers became aware that in water, a small electric current may float between the lead, and a hook made of carbon steel. It was theorised that after getting hooked when picking up a bait in an area in which this current was detected, a fish may learn to avoid hook-baits. Mike Wilson first mentioned this to me at least 8 years ago, and I believe anglers had been coating their leads some time before that. I suppose coating the lead does no harm. It's one of those many little instances of attention to detail, the sum total of which may, in the end, make a difference. I don't doubt carp's ability to detect small amounts of electrical activity, but as that is how, in some instances they find their food (ionisation) I wonder if it could attract rather than repel them! I say that with my tongue firmly in my cheek, as I don't know enough about under-water physics to argue the point. What coating does very well however, is to camouflage the lead. I think it more likely a fish will be put off by the fact that every time he picks a bait in the vicinity of a shiny lump of metal, he has a nasty experience, than by minuscule amounts of electrical activity. Mind you, they keep on doing it don't they! Again it must depend on how much pressure your water has seen, and how many fish are in it. On an overstocked hungry water, it probably wouldn't make any difference: on a rich, low stocked and highly pressured water, a camouflaged lead may help. You can buy the coating powder: on it, then re-heat until an even coating has formed. After melting a few leads you'll probably get the hang of it! I wouldn't worry too much about coating leads if you have several feet of soft silt on the bed of the lake you are fishing!

As an alternative to coating your lead, or as additional insurance if you are concerned about electrical currents flowing between hook and lead, you could use the Partridge Grey Shadow hooks with their Niflor coating.

It is also said that coating leads protects them from damage by gravel bars. Well I don't know what the people who say that are coating their leads with! My coatings last about one day when fishing the bars, ending up flapping around like flags after two or three casts! I think one should also consider the possibility that an unevenly coated lead may offer more air resistance in the cast. Lead coating powder comes in various colours and is now available from most good tackle shops. It was originally available from Keith Selleck of the Middlesex Angling Centre, and if you have trouble obtaining some, give him a ring.

OTHER CASTING AIDS

Casting aids other than leads are almost totally confined to rigs used in fishing surface baits, or floaters as they are better known. Though leads can be used quite successfully for fishing floaters, most anglers now use some form of controller. I used to make my own, as in the Diagram , but there are now many

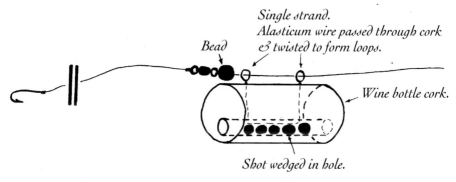

Single strand.
Alasticum wire passed through cork
Bead &3 twisted to form loops.

Wine bottle cork.

Shot wedged in hole.

Home made controller.

excellent commercial versions available, most being basically a weighted float which enables the bait to be cast out. These are generally known as controllers. Kevin Nash produces these in two different sizes, and Pete Drennan offers a good range which, being transparent, are quite inconspicuous in water. Then there are the Terry Eustace floater floats, a unique item and part of Terry's excellent 'Gold Label' range. They are rather like a large self cocking waggler float, with a swivel in the top to pass the line through. Their main advantage is that they have a large sight bob which stands well clear of the water, and is easily visible at some distance.

There is another type of controller made by Gardner, and called the 'Suspender'. This holds the line off the surface in the vicinity of the bait, leaving only the hook and hookbait for the fish to see. I was a bit annoyed when Gardner brought this out, as , after much trial and error, I had just perfected my own version!

Another clever device made by Gardner is their 'Mixer Fixer', a controller which you can fill up with free offerings. After being cast out, these emerge around the hookbait.

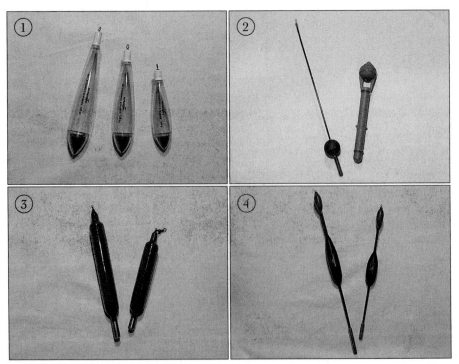

1. Drennan controllers.   2. Gardner Suspender and Mixer Fixer
3. Nash Controllers.   4. Terry Eustace controllers.

TANGLES/ANTI-TANGLE AIDS

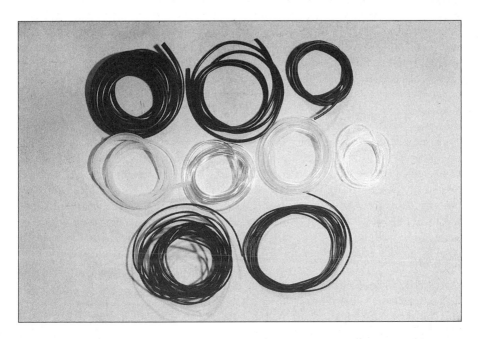

Anti-tangle tubing was first used in the early to mid-eighties, and has been successful in preventing tangles caused by the hook-link wrapping around the main line behind the lead. This is simply because the tubing is far thicker than the main line, and the tangles do not so easily occur; or if they do, they will often untwist as the tackle is sinking. Feathering the cast down for the last few yards will help to minimise these tangles, with or without tubing. Another source of tangles when using normal leads, that is leads which hang at right angles to the line, is the link between the line and the lead, around which the hook-link often catches. This can be minimised by pushing tubing over the link, and soft, flexible tubing is best for this.

Like many items of a carp fisher's equipment nowadays, there is a bewildering choice of anti-tangle tubing available. The main differences are colour, size and stiffness. The choice between any one of them though is not purely arbitrary. Anti-tangle tubing is made from different types of materials. Broadly speaking, one type is soft and rubbery, while the other is more shiny, and harder. Also, some is very stiff, while other types are quite flexible. If you wish to fish a running ledger, then I would advise that you use the shiny type, of which Kevin Nash produces a good range, which includes a very fine diameter PTFE tubing. The reason I recommend this is that line tends to stick in the rubbery tubing, even to some extent when it is wet, and it probably won't give the total lack of resistance you are trying to achieve by using a running lead. The same will also apply to back-stopped rigs, though this may not be so important; and of course, if you are using fixed leads, it won't matter at all.

The tube comes in varying thicknesses, and whilst I doubt internal bore size has any great significance, though the narrower tube may in some instances offer more resistance to the line passing through it, outside diameter does. The thicker and longer your tubing, the more it will restrict your casting distance, but the more effective an anti-tangle aid it will be. Always remember that to be effective the tubing must be some inches longer than your hook-link. Thinner diameter tubing may be less conspicuous to the fish, won't make so much difference to the cast, but may be less likely to prevent tangles. I prefer to use the flexible tube, as the stiff tubing, being very straight, and almost invariably black, looks very unnatural to me. There don't seem to be many objects in nature that are truly black, or dead straight. Consider how obvious a fishing rod looks, even from some distance, poking out from the margins of a reedy lake. If you like using stiff tubing, have a look at the almost clear stuff Pete Drennan makes. Whichever you go for, try to ensure that once cast out, the tubing will lie on the bottom, and not stick up at an angle. I think this is most likely to occur with the comet leads, if you are fishing over a soft bottom where the lead will sink in. Pulling back a few inches will solve the problem.

Twenty+ taken on a critically balanced pop-up and fixed lead.

For a while there was tubing available with lead at both ends in an attempt to overcome this. I think the problem was greatly exaggerated, as, even if the tubing is filled with air, after a short time in the water, much of the air will leak out, and the weight of the line will ensure the tube lays on the bottom. The weight of the tubing itself will also have an effect on this. If you have any doubts about the sinking rate of the tubing you are using, try it in your bath. If it floats, and this bothers you then attach a weight to the end of it.

I'm not sure that colour is that important, except that when everyone was using thick black tubing, I did try to find alternatives, both in diameter, and colour. I used the outer sleeve from individual strands of 5 amp wire (lighting cable), and used it in the colours it came in, that is black or red, or sprayed it with matt brown and green paint, giving it a good airing to let the paint smell fade before using it. This is quite heavy, and sinks to the bottom quickly. I also had some fine diameter tubing given to me that was coloured bright green. I have caught fish on all of these, though I always feel more confident using tubing of a colour that may match any bits of weed or stick that may be laying around on the lake bed. There is of course the possible benefit that tubing of the right colour may actually disguise the line.

I am at present using a fine diameter flexible tube which is coloured dark green. I don't know who makes it, but I know Ritchie MacDonald at the Hounslow Angling Centre can supply it, and it is also available in brown. E.T. Products also produce a green coloured tube, in various diameters, as well as a fairly comprehensive range of other tubing. I haven't seen any of their products so can make no further comment on them.

Stiff tube

Round bead

Anti-tangle rig using single spigotted 'Roberts' bead & short piece of stiff tubing to create a boom.

If I am trying to fish with a minimum of resistance, I try to do without the tubing behind the lead, and feather the cast. I do though use a short piece of stiffish tubing, about an inch long, in front of the lead, and affixed to a spigotted Roberts type bead. This acts as a small boom, and helps keep the hook-link away from the main line during the cast. Because I am aiming to fish without resistance, in this case I push a length of narrower tubing up inside the original piece to prevent the swivel becoming stuck in the tube. You could use a small bead for this if you prefer.

An alternative to anti-tangle tubing is to use a short length of lead cored fly-line. This can be tied to the main line with a needle knot, and this is a very neat way of joining fly-line to mono. It is not an easy knot to tie on the bank though, and it is easier just to peel the plastic coating to the braid, strip out some of the lead, and use a double Grinner.

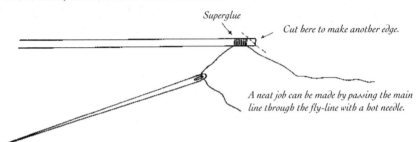

Superglue

Cut here to make another edge.

A neat job can be made by passing the main line through the fly-line with a hot needle.

The fly-line can be fastened to the swivel in a similar manner. Using lead-cored line has the advantage that it will always lie on the bottom, but it may restrict you to the use of fixed leads, as the knots joining it to the main line and the hook-link will be quite bulky, preventing the rig from running freely. You can buy short lengths of lead-core from the Middlesex Angling Centre, whose lines don't have any plastic coating, or you can buy a whole flyline from any tackle shop, and cut it up yourself. There are fly-lines, and fly-lines - don't buy a Cortland - ask for a cheap line, or a mill-end.

P.V.A. - Poly-Vinyl Alcohol - is a great anti-tangle aid. For the very few of you who don't know what P.V.A. is, it is a stretchy polythene-like material which dissolves in water. It dissolves quicker in warm water than in cold, and can now be bought in different grades, where melting times are stated according to water temperature. You can buy it in several forms - tape, string, bags and tubes, and it has many applications, but probably the most frequent use is for tying on stringers, which I'll come to in the rig section. There are anglers I know who won't use P.V.A. because they believe the carp can detect the smell. There are others who won't use it in case it causes pollution, and I respect that view without knowing if there is any truth in it. There must be an awful lot of it going into our lakes - does anyone know whether it dissolves completely? As to the first point, whether the carp can detect it or not, an enormous amount of carp are caught on rigs that have included the use of P.V.A., so I don't think you can ignore it. There may however, be a market for flavoured P.V.A.! P.V.A. string is the most useful for avoiding tangles, enabling you to tie up all the loose ends in your rig before casting out. When I am using the hair, I always tie the bait tight to the shank with P.V.A. before casting. I then stretch the loose end of the P.V.A. between hook point and hook-link, effectively closing the gape and preventing the hook catching on anything. It will also enable you to cast long hook-links, possibly without tubing, by bunching them up and tying them with P.V.A. string.

A recent development from Kryston is a sticky substance called 'No-Tangle'. This also dissolves in water, is non-toxic and was intended initially for use with multi-stranded hook-links such as the Kryston multi-strand. A small drop applied along the length of the hook-link and worked in with the fingers will, after approximately one minute in the air, dry and stiffen the hook-link, sticking together the individual strands. This greatly reduces the risk of tangles on the cast, and totally dissolves after about a minute in the water. Even then, it does to some extent prevent the strands separating, and thereby helps reduce the underwater tangles which occur when twigs and creatures become caught up in the strands. It can also be used with the Gamabraids and the Kryston braids, with the exception of Supersilk, which is too tightly woven to allow the gel to be worked in. Stiffening line is not all it does however; given time, it will stick most things together, even baits, and therefore has many applications for the imaginative angler.

Kryston are bringing out a new version of the 'No-Tangle' which will stiffen braids almost to the consistency of a wire trace. It takes a bit longer to dry than the original gel but should make tangles a thing of the past.

Some rigs have been specifically designed to avoid tangles, and one of the best of these is the helicopter rig, named such because the hook-link is free to swivel around the main line like a helicopter rotor. This is described in more detail in the section on rigs.

SWIVELS/BEADS

There's not much I can say about the plain swivel other than that I always use Berkley swivels for joining my hook-link to the main line. I have found them totally reliable in every situation in which I have used them and don't know of a better swivel; everyone I know uses them.

   Link swivels are used primarily in carp fishing for attaching the lead to the line, giving you an easy method of changing leads, or, on rods that are left permanently set up, removing the lead when carrying the rods about. Whilst I would again only use the Berkley link swivels if I was actually attaching a hook-link to them as I do when pike fishing, where the link swivel is used purely as a means of attaching the lead I have found any make to be suitable. Using swivels for this purpose has largely been superseded by the use of a 'Roberts' type bead, with a small snap-link attached to it.

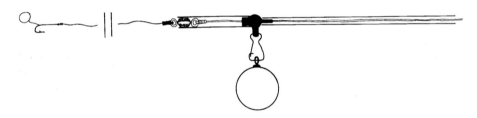

Bolt rig set up using double spigotted bead, & snap link.
Hook-link swivel is pushed into tubing.

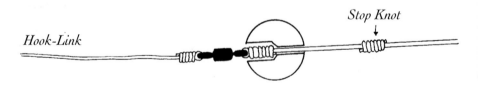

Dual bored bead. One end protects knot, other end stops 'stop knot' passing through.

The bead has progressed from its humble beginnings, and is no longer necessarily just a round thing with a hole in it. The round ones come in all colours and sizes, floating and sinking. Some have a small diameter hole bored through them, which is useful for interposing between stop-knots and wide bore tubing. The small bore beads won't however offer a normal knot much protection, and if you feel this is necessary it is best to use a large bored bead that will sit over the knot. Many years ago I had some small beads which were bored halfway through with a big hole, and the other half with a small hole. Both Drennan shock beads and Kevin Nash knot beads are bored in this manner, and offer the best of both worlds.

The first deviation from the round bead was invented by John Roberts, and is now commonly known as the 'Roberts' bead. These have a large hole at the top, to fit over your line, or tubing, and a small hole at the bottom which you can use to attach the lead, normally by means of a small snap-link. Anglers used to use link-swivels for this purpose, but there was always the worry that the narrow metal eye of the swivel would damage the line. The 'Roberts' beads have a much broader area in contact with the line and are less likely to cause damage. Later versions of these beads have a spigot either at one end, or both ends, onto which you can push your anti-tangle tube. Others just have a hole large enough for you to slide the bead over the tube, which is better if you are using very stiff tubing. Swivel beads, as their name implies, have a small swivel to which you can attach your lead, and this can be useful when using running ledgers, and may also, to some extent, help prevent tangles on the cast. You can get them from Kevin Nash or Pete Drennan.

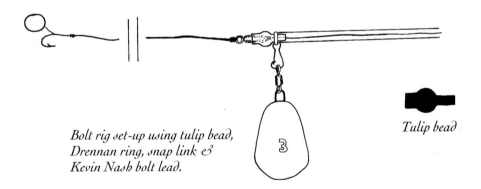

Bolt rig set-up using tulip bead, Drennan ring, snap link & Kevin Nash bolt lead.

Tulip bead

In between the original bead, and the Roberts bead are the tulip beads, presumably named so because they are roughly similar in shape to a tulip head. These are set up as in the Diagram 5, and have an advantage in that they enable you to get the lead close to the line, enhancing the bolt rig effect, and reducing the risk of tangles that occur when the hook-link wraps round the lead link. Beads being generally so small, I doubt if colour matters that much, but if it worries you, Drennan make beads to cover just about every situation, and like most of their end tackle bits, they are transparent with either a tint of green, or brown.

Alan with a mid double caught on a critically balanced hair rig pop-up.

SHOCK/SNAG LEADERS

A shack leader is a heavy length of line (11lb-25lb b.s. +) connecting the main line to the hook length. There are two reasons for using a shock leader. One is to enable you to use fine running line, the shock leader taking the strain of the cast. This is how 'shock leaders' originally got their name - they take the shock from heavy casting, enabling the angler to use light running line and therefore allowing longer casts than would be possible if heavy line were used straight through. In this case, the length of the leader need only be about one and a half times the length of the rod. Breaking strain should be related to the size of lead being used, and in most practical carp fishing situations, leaders of 15-20lb breaking strain will suffice.

The other reason for using leaders heavier than the main line is to prevent cut offs on gravel bars, or snags. Again lines of 15-20lb will cover most situations, though I do know of a pit where anglers were using leaders of 60lbs b.s. and still getting cut off on the bars! If the line pulls directly across a sharp edge, such as a mussel, then probably nothing short of a wire trace is going to save you! This however is not a practical solution - even if you could cast a sufficient length of trace, I doubt a set of rod rings would last long, especially after playing a few heavy fish! I have used wire in the set up, when I was fishing a lake where I was getting cut offs from swan mussels embedded in the silt. The line would invariably break up to a foot behind the swivel; a yard of 20lb Berkley Marlinsteel cured that problem. I suppose I could have used tubing, but it wasn't 'invented' then!

The length of a snag leader will depend on how deep the water is, and how near the surface the snags, or gravel bars are, and how far out you are fishing. To illustrate, if your water is 5 feet deep, and you are fishing over one bar which is 6 feet wide, and comes within 2 feet of the surface, you probably won't need a very long leader. If your line is lying across several bars, or if you are fishing deep water where the bars come within a foot of the surface, then your leader must be long enough to ensure that none of your main line touches the bars WHEN UNDER TENSION.

Some lines have more resistance to abrasion than others. Some good ones are Maxima, Sylcast and Brent. Slightly better is Trilene XT (stands for extra tough), though there is now a new line available from Trilene which in tests has proved up to 5 times more abrasion resistant than other makes. This is Trilene Big Game line, available from Terry Eustace. It comes in 12lb, 15lb and 20lb breaking strains, and should be available in 10lb b.s. by the time this book is published. Those breaking strains appear to be understated by around 15-20%. Unlike most other abrasion resistant lines, 'Big Game' has little memory; that is, when it comes off the spool, it lays flat and doesn't stay in little coils. Because of its increased resistance to abrasion over other lines, and its relatively fine diameter, in many situations you can use it straight through, especially in the 12 and 15lb breaking strains. If you can get away with it, this is always preferable to using a leader, especially when fishing near snags where, if your line does break, it often goes at the leader knot, leaving the fish towing long lengths of heavy line.

Using the 12lb 'Big Game' straight through is probably better than, or at least as good as using 10lb main line with a 20lb leader of any other monofilament. If you want to use finer running line, and are using the leader purely as a shock leader, then the 12lb b.s. will be sufficient, as tests have shown that 'Big Game' line has 100% energy absorption, this compared to 67% in Maxima. I have been using the 12lbs b.s. straight through for pike fishing, and casting heavy dead-baits a long way with no problems; that is an excellent test for a shock leader. 'Big Game' is reasonably fine for its breaking strain, and is colourless. If you wish you can easily dye line for leaders, if not main line, and I expect many carp anglers will be using it before long.

Kryston multi-strand is well-known for its incredible abrasion resistance, and though this is of limited use in a hook-link, Kryston have now developed a braided version of the multi-strand called 'Quick-Silver'. This is intended for use in shock leaders, and comes in breaking strains of 25lb and 45lb. It is very fine for its strength, and is dyed permanent brown. I'm not sure what its energy absorption rate is, but in those breaking strains, I doubt if it matters much. The 25lb is roughly the same diameter as 12lb dacron, and the 45lb about the same as 15lb dacron. I have carried out abrasion resistance tests on these, with surprising results. I initially tried them across the edge of a brick, with a 2lb lead weight attached to the line. After over 100 strokes, I decided to try something different! I then tested them, again with a 2lb lead attached, by pulling the line back and forward across the serrated edge of a bread knife! The 25lb broke after 58 strokes, and the 45lb after 110 strokes. The toughest mono I had tested just 3 strokes! If you are having serious problems with line cutting, then using Trilene Big Game as a main line coupled with a Quick-silver leader should solve those problems. Quick-silver should be on the market by the time this book is published. The only drawback I can see with using it is that it may not go through the rod rings as easily as mono, and might therefore effect casting distance. However, as I haven't actually fished with it, I can't confirm that.

For joining leaders to main line, I don't think you can better the double Grinner knot already mentioned, though you can experiment with the number of turns. Generally you will find that the thicker the line, the less turns you need to make. If I was tying a 20lb leader to 10lb main line, I would probably make 2 or 3 turns with the thicker line, and 4 or 5 with the thinner.

The only other reliable knot I might use for joining two lengths of line is the four-turn water knot.

Always test your leader knots carefully at the start of a session; they have a habit of sometimes weakening overnight. I know some anglers superglue the knot, and this probably helps.

One last thing on leaders, which most of you probably know anyway: before casting, make sure the knot is positioned at the back of the spool. If it is anywhere else, line will catch on it when you cast. At best you will lose distance on the cast; at worst you will break off.

BALANCING AIDS

One last component of the rig to mention before going on to the rigs themselves is the materials used to sink, or balance, buoyant baits. Initially, most anglers used lead shot, though I know some anglers were not happy about doing so, as they felt it may weaken the hook-link. I never had any problems with the soft lead shot, but since this has been made illegal, and the new non-toxic shots are much harder, I have tried alternatives. It depends largely on what sort of hook-link I am using. If I am using either dacron, Silkworm or Merlin in their heavier breaking strains, I often use the non-toxic shot, though I am fussy about which make I choose. One of the best, that is softest, is Anchor shot, and I use this frequently. If I am using fine hook-links, or multi-strand, then I use either small diameter tubing pushed on the line, and push 'lead' wire inside it, or lead putty. The latter is an excellent balancing aid, enabling you to critically balance the bait. The only problem I find with it is that it can make a mess of multi-strand, and being lighter than lead, it can require an awfully big lump of it to balance a really buoyant bait.

What I do in practice is to use a combination of the above, depending on the situation. I may use a non-toxic shot for the main weight. then finely balance it by adding lead putty. There are several makes of lead putty available, and E.T. Products produce it in a range of colours. I don't think colour is so important, but try to get one that doesn't smell! Some work better than others, and the one I am currently using is supplied by Gardner tackle, and seems quite good. What I especially like about the Gardner putty is that it comes in a little plastic tub, and not a plastic bag which allows a used packet to collect all your pocket fluff!

The use of a buoyant bait with a balancing weight on the hook-link will probably help make it more difficult for the carp to eject the bait, as it will cause an imbalance in the rig when the fish picks up the bait. The distance between the balancing weight and hook will also have some influence on this. I have often thought of attaching the balancing weight to the spare end of he knot.

This would create a further imbalance, and also allow you to use non-toxic shot as a balance weight without fear of it damaging the hook-link itself. In some instances, using more weight than is necessary to balance the bait could also be to advantage, the weight tending to pull the hook downwards in the carp's mouth , thereby to some extent negating the bait's buoyancy.

It is obviously quite possible for a carp to suck and blow at a bait and hook without either coming in contact with the inside of the fish's mouth. The addition of a balance weight relatively close to the hook may help upset the smoothness of that operation.

Alternative position of balance weight for pop-up.

RIGS

BASIC PRINCIPLES/CONSIDERATIONS

The basic idea of a rig is to present a bait to a fish in such a manner that it will pick up that bait, and either hook itself, or give the angler sufficient indication to enable him to set the hook himself. There are many ways to achieve this depending largely on the behaviour of the carp in your water. Rigs can be split into two groups, the confidence rigs, and the bolt rigs. There may be some overlapping here, and at times, they may function in completely the opposite way in which you intend them to; after all, screaming runs were quite common in the days of the ultimate confidence rig, the freelined paste with the hook hidden inside it. And who has not had the occasional slow and confident take when using a fixed lead?

This could of course spark off a debate as to why carp run, and though there may be more than one reason for this, when setting up a rig which is intended to make a carp run, it is assumed the fish will run because it has sensed something abnormal, and panicked. Some carp may be more sensitive in this respect than others adding yet another variable to the logarithm!

There are some rigs that combine the two principles intentionally, allowing the fish to pick up the bait and move off a short distance without arousing its suspicions, but then giving it a shock, or jolt. Back-stopped rigs are a good example of this, and if you are fishing with a closed bale-arm, that might have the same effect. Other rigs are adjusted so that the fish will hook itself as soon as it picks up the bait, and to achieve this the length of the hook-link is critical. Yet others are designed to enable the carp to swim off with the bait unsuspecting, until the angler strikes. In most cases nowadays it would seem desirable to get the fish to run, and I think this is what most anglers are trying to achieve. This is perhaps as much a reflection on angler's behaviour as that of the carp. Long gone are the days when carp anglers would sit up all night watching dough bobbins or pieces of silver paper though bleary eyes, waiting to hit the slightest twitch. Now we want to do it in comfort - let the carp hook itself while we snooze mummified in best quality sleeping bags inside expensive designer carp houses! If we had to go back to sitting up all night hitting twitches, I think 90% of carp anglers would disappear! Perhaps we may have to yet!

Any rig is obviously made up of different components, and these may be combined in many different ways; for example, any one method of attaching a bait to a hook may be fished on a long or short hook-link, and with a large or small lead which may be fixed, or not. The bait may be buoyant, critically balanced or a normal bait. The hook-link may be fully or partly straightened after casting, or not straightened at all. It may also be made from a combination of materials, a very effective arrangement being 8 inches of mono, and 4 inches of multi-strand, which also helps prevent tangles. Main line may be slack, back-leaded or clipped up tight. The fish may be picking up baits in their lips and moving off, or sucking and blowing them from up to a foot away. The direction from which a fish approaches your bait may also have some bearing on whether you hook that fish or not, though that is likely to be beyond your control.

The author with a 19+ caught on a top hooked boilie.

ATTACHING HOOK TO BAIT

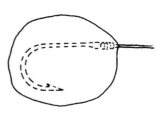

Hook hidden in bait.

PRE-HAIR RIG

Hook in Bait

One of the first things carp anglers began to do in an attempt to allay the suspicions of the carp was to start hiding the hooks in the bait. You can imagine that the baits had to be very soft to give the angler any chance of hooking the fish, and I speak from experience when I say that even then, you would often pull both bait and hook from the fish's mouth without hooking it. In the early days this was something of a tragedy, as there weren't many carp about, and chances were few and far between.

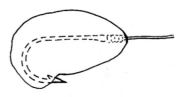

Hookpoint exposed.

Hook point out

Leaving the hook-point exposed provided a partial answer, but the use of soft baits brought other problems in the shape of nuisance fish - usually bream and tench, or smaller fish that would whittle the bait away to nothing while the angler sat uncertain whether or not to strike at the continuous twitches. In an effort to avoid the nuisance fish, anglers began using harder baits, but as hiding most of the hook was still sacrosanct, anglers still had difficulty in hooking fish, as the hooks would not pull through the hard baits. This in turn put many people off using hard baits, and they persevered with the softer pastes, and all their inherent problems.

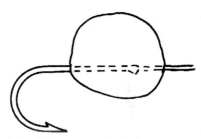

Side hooking: correct bait size.

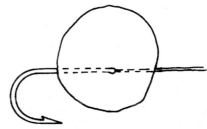

Side hooking: Hook point masked by too large a bait.

Side Hooking /
Top Hooking

I don't know who first did it, but eventually someone took the bold step of just nicking the hook into the bait, leaving the greater part of it exposed. This was immediately successful, shot around the incredible carp grapevine, and soon most carp anglers were fishing using these methods, which became known as side-hooking and top-hooking. I don't know which came first, but the basic difference is that a side-hooked bait is mounted at the back of the shank, near or over the eye, while a top-hooked bait is nicked on to hang just below the bend. If you are using these methods, obviously consideration must be given to the size of hook you use; it is of little use mounting a 1 inch bait on a size 8 hook in this manner. For optimum effect the size of the hook gape should be roughly similar to the diameter of the bait or you will greatly reduce your chances of hooking the fish, though you can get away with a smaller hook if you are top-hooking so long as you nick it lightly into the bait.

One unfortunate variation of these rigs which should be mentioned for the sake of completeness was the (un-named?) one in which the bait was slid up the hook-link, and the hook tied on afterwards. As far as I know, this had limited success and anglers soon dropped it as many of the fish caught on it were foul-hooked. There is a more recent variation of this in which the hook floats above the bait. I don't know of anyone who uses it, but have found it prone to tangle on the few occasions I have tried it.

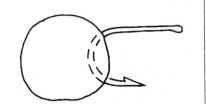

Top hooking: Larger bait assists self hooking on bait rigs.

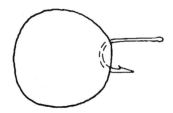

Smaller hook can be used as long as it will pull out of bait on strike

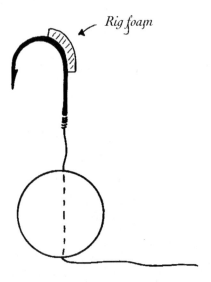

Rig foam

Hook floating above bait.

John Read with a lovely scattered mirror of 27.11 caught on hair rig particle.
Below. John Miles with a pop-up caught mirror of 22lb+

HAIR AND VARIATIONS

After the initial wave of success, results on the side-hooking and top-hooking methods began to slow down. It was seen that the carp were eating the free offerings and leaving the hookbait. Either they were seeing the line coming from the bait, feeling it across their lips when they picked up the hook bait, or detecting the difference in weight of the bait with the hook in it as compared to a free offering. The hair-rig as originally conceived by Lenny Middleton was an attempt to solve the former of the afore mentioned problems, and it did so incredibly successfully. In the original rig the bait was attached to the bend of the hook by a single strand of human hair. After pulling all their own hair out, he and his friends began using fine nylon with equal success (now you know why so many old carp anglers are bald!). The hair-rig also helped solve the second problem by allowing the use of smaller hooks, and had another beneficial effect in that it operated as an anti-eject mechanism, and could therefore be used in bolt rigs as well as the confidence rigs for which it had originally been designed. It had yet another advantage in preventing the bite-offs some anglers were experiencing when confidently feeding carp were taking the bait into their pharyngeal teeth, and in the act of crushing the bait

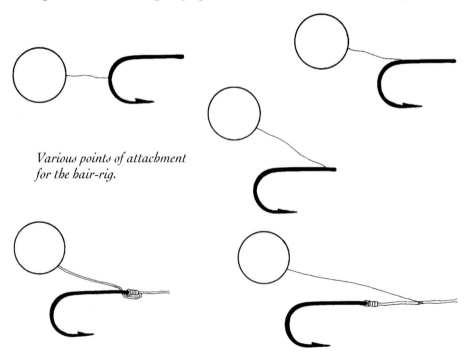

Various points of attachment for the hair-rig.

60

were also crushing the line.

The basic concept of the hair spawned numerous variations of that principle, some designed to overcome a specific problem, and some purely for experiment.

The main variations when using a hair-rig are the point of attachment to the hook, hair length, hair material and whether the hair is actually fixed to the hook, or allowed to move about, as in the 'D' rig where the hair may slide up and down making it more difficult for the fish to eject the bait. You also have

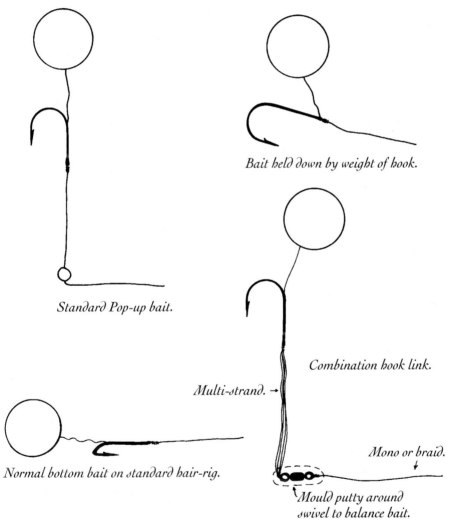

Bait held down by weight of hook.

Standard Pop-up bait.

Combination hook link.

Multi-strand. →

Mono or braid.
↓

Normal bottom bait on standard hair-rig.

Mould putty around swivel to balance bait.

the choice of attaching the bait by tying the hair around its outside, which is best done using a dental floss hair, or passing it through the bait using a baiting needle.

The original hair-rig had the hair tied to the bottom of the hook bend. Anglers soon began to investigate ways of increasing the rig's efficiency by attaching it elsewhere, either to the the eye, or coming straight down in line with the shank. Other anglers actually attached it to the hook-link, up to an inch above the eye. This particular rig was known as the Spring rig (see illustration) and utilised a smallish hook, and a stiff hook link, though I'm not sure what advantage this was meant to confer. All of these variations of the theme worked to some extent, though I don't know that it was ever proved

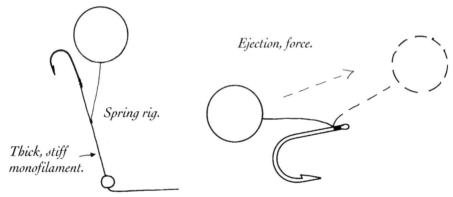

Spring rig.

Thick, stiff monofilament.

Ejection, force.

Hair attatched to hook eye may work better as an anti-eject rig.

conclusively that one way offered any great advantage over another.

Hair length was generally related to the size of the fish, and more specifically to the distance between their lips and pharyngeal teeth, being calculated so that when the bait was in the teeth, the hook would be inside the lips. The most efficient length seemed to be somewhere between $^3/_4$ inch and $1^1/_2$ inches, but it is important that the length of the hair is also related to bait and hook size. You will realise it is of little use fishing a 1 inch bait attached by a very short hair to a size 12 hook. Equally, if you are using a small bait and a long hair, there would seem little point in using a a large and heavy hook unless you particularly wish to do so. Generally, the longer the hair, the smaller the hook can be, and the shorter the hair, the larger it will need to be.

If you set up a hair-rig by passing the hair through a small piece of fine diameter rig tubing, then slipping this over the hook, the point of attachment to the hook can be instantly varied by sliding the tube to different positions on the shank. If the upper end of the hair is passed through the hook eye, then tied to the main line, hair length can be adjusted by sliding this knot up and down.

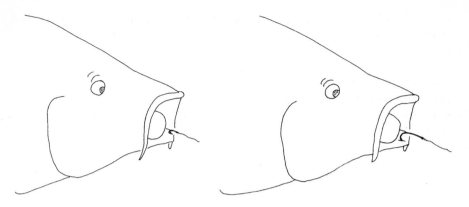

1. *Bait is too large for small hook &*
short hair; easily ejected without hook
catching up.

2. *Same bait & hair, but larger hook*
giving more chance of it catching up.

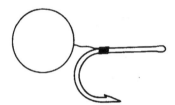

Small bait more effective on short hair.

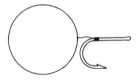

Bait too large for short hair – may be
ejected without hook catching up.

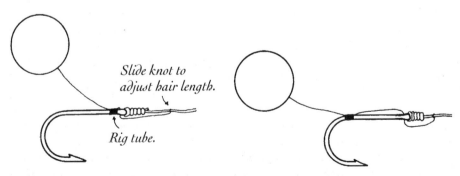

Set up of adjustable hair: Tubing can be slid along shank to vary position. Hair can
be lengthened, or shortened by sliding knot along hair-link.

The bait was initially attached to the hair by threading the line through it, and tying it on. This wasn't very efficient, as it meant you had to tie on a new hair every time you changed the bait. Anglers began tying small loops in the end of the hair and after pulling this through the bait with a baiting needle, kept it in place with some form of boilie stop. In those days this was usually a piece of twig or something similar. Now there is no need to hunt through the undergrowth looking for a suitable material - there are several versions available commercially, and some of the best are the little dumb-bell shaped ones made by Kevin Nash, Drennan's 'bone' shaped ones, and the plastic stripes which you can bite a groove in, which Terry Eustace sells.

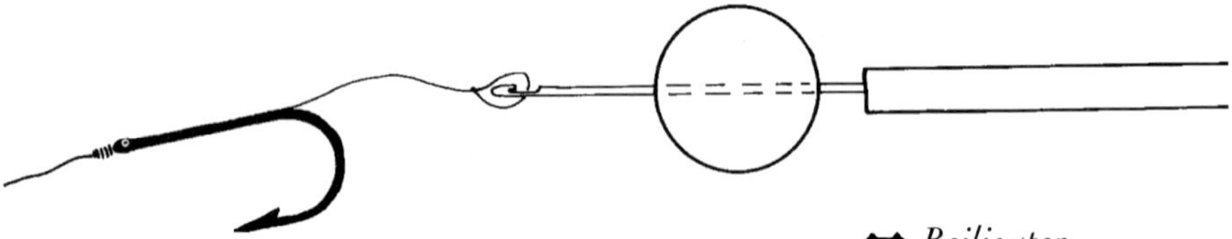

Boilie stop.

Using small baiting needle & boilie stop to mount bait.

Whilst the fine line used for the hair was successful, it did have a problem in that when fished with a heavy fixed lead, or tight line clips, some nuisance fish were capable of breaking the hair, and making off with the bait giving the angler little or no indication that this had happened. Some anglers began to use dacron or dental floss for the hair, and this was also successful, but did have a drawback in that it made a larger hole in the bait, allowing it to become water-logged in a relatively short time (though it has to be said that this can happen when using fine line for the hair, which tends to cut into the bait, thereby enlarging the hole). With the critically balanced baits, i.e. those balanced so they just sink, this is a problem. It can be overcome by either sealing the holes with a small drop of superglue, or tying the bait onto the floss without actually making a hole in it, but by looping the floss around it. This is better done after wetting the floss, and be sure to tie plenty of knots - dental floss has a nasty habit of coming undone. To help prevent the bait slipping out, you can soak it in water for a short while before casting out, where it will expand and tighten the floss; or you can make your hook-baits with a small groove around them for the floss to sit in. If you go for the superglue method you will find superglue gel far more manageable than the other stuff; you may even be able to seal the bait up without gluing it to your fingers! The diameter of the baiting needle you use to pull line through the bait also has some bearing on the amount of water absorbed, so try to use the thinnest needle possible.

There are several versions of baiting needle available commercially, but they are all too thick for my liking, so I make my own from fine sewing needles.

Baits tied tight to Drennan ring using dental floss.

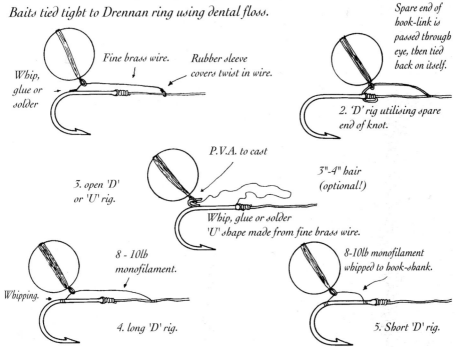

Fine brass wire.

Rubber sleeve covers twist in wire.

Whip, glue or solder

Spare end of hook-link is passed through eye, then tied back on itself.

2. 'D' rig utilising spare end of knot.

P.V.A. to cast

3"-4" hair (optional!)

3. open 'D' or 'U' rig.

Whip, glue or solder 'U' shape made from fine brass wire.

8 - 10lb monofilament.

8-10lb monofilament whipped to hook-shank.

Whipping.

4. long 'D' rig.

5. Short 'D' rig.

Variations on the 'D' rig. Designed to leave hook in carp's mouth when it ejects bait.

The 'D' rig was probably the first of several rigs designed to make it more difficult for the fish to eject the bait. The basic principle is that when a carp tries to blow the bait out, the hair will slide along the 'D' allowing the bait to move, but not the hook. There are several rigs now based on this principle, all of which are shown in the rig diagrams. I have used my own version of this rig, which I suppose you could call the open 'D' rig. Basically, you only use half a 'D' and this is made from a small piece of brass wire which, after being whipped onto the back of the hookshank, is bent into a 'U' shape, the top of the 'U' facing the eye. A small Drennan ring is tied to the bait using dental floss, and a long hair tied to the ring. The other end of the hair is then tied to the eye of the hook, and the bait positioned close to the hook by sliding the ring over the wire, and held in place for the cast with P.V.A. The idea is that when ejected by the carp, the hook won't move at all until the hair is fully straightened. The only reason the hair is there is so that , if something moves the rig and separates bait and hook, at least you will be fishing with a bait

The author with a lighty scaled mirror of over 25lbs.

Carp sucks in bait on 'U' rig.

Carp ejects bait – hook & bait separate leaving hook in carp's mouth.

attached. If you are really brave, don't use the hair at all! For obvious reasons I don't recommend leaving this rig out for long periods, and I would recommend you use a set-up that will let you know if the bait is moved. If you do try this without the hair, and you use a bait big and bright enough for you to see it then there is the interesting possibility of you knowing that a carp has ejected the bait, as it should bob up to the surface, as long as nothing snaffles it on the way up! This is obviously not a ploy for long sessions, or long range, and in any case, with luck you would know a fish had taken the bait by the excited state of your indicators!

The 'D' rig and its variations are all best used with pop-ups, or buoyant baits, as this ensures the bait is sitting at the right end of the hook, that is, the bend. If you fish a normal bottom bait it may slide down near the eye, resulting in the hook going into the carp's mouth the wrong way round when it picks up the bait.

One other rig worth mentioning is the sliding hair-rig, first publicised by Rod Hutchinson. An illustration can be found in the rig diagrams, and this rig was designed for fishing bottom baits to wary fish, though I suppose you could get away with fishing a pop-up on it as long as you put the balance weight on the hair, below the hook. The idea is that the carp can suck the bait into its mouth initially without the hook moving, as the hair slides along the hook-link. This gives the fish the idea the bait is not attached to anything, and it then takes the bait in properly, but this time, all the play in the sliding hair having been taken up, the hook goes in as well. The loop on the hair should be P.V.A.'d to the hook-link for casting.

Some anglers have dispensed with the supple hairs altogether, and attach a bait by pushing a stiff bristle through it, this bristle being secured to the hook shank. The theory is that the bristle will bend as the fish tries to eject the bait, making it more difficult for the carp to do so.

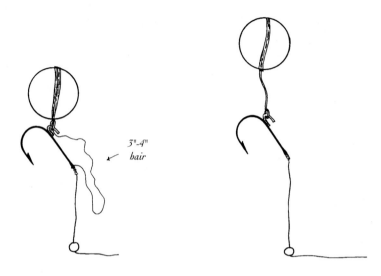

*3"-4"
hair*

Variations on the open 'D' or 'U' rig.

Looped hair rig for floaters.

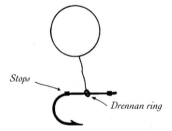

Stops

Drennan ring

Revolving hair-rig.

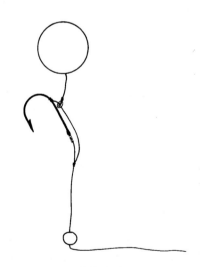

A variation of the 'D' rig.

loose loop

Pop-up on sliding hair.

Sliding hair rig: bottom baits only.

'D' rigs are best fished with 'pop-up' baits, ensuring hook goes in carp's mouth the right way round (fig. a). If fished with bottom baits, hook may enter the carp's mouth back to front (fig. b).

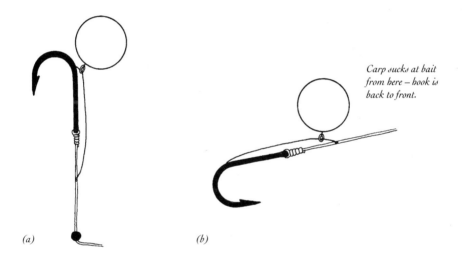

Carp sucks at bait from here – hook is back to front.

(a)   (b)

A vaguely similar method of mounting the bait is the Drennan boilie bayonet. This is a stretchy piece of rubber, having a ring at one end, and a 'bayonet' on which to impale your baits at the other. This bayonet has several small 'barbs' to prevent the bait slipping off. It has to be tied or whipped to the hook, or can be fixed with fine diameter tubing. You can then either use the bayonet, or the ring to affix your baits. Though the bayonet has the advantage of convenience, the main drawback is the amount of water it will let into the bait, and if you are using buoyant baits, you might have to change them frequently. The make up of the bait itself will affect this, as the hole made by the bayonet may, to some extent be self sealing in a fine bait, such as a milk protein, but ragged in the coarser fish meals and bird foods, thereby allowing the entry of more water around its edges. The bayonet may also be difficult to use with very hard baits.

For those interested in this system of bait mounting, Marvic are also introducing a similar system - their boilie spike, which is a kind of plastic peg which is attached to the hair, and again pushed into the bait. It might be an idea for someone to make something similar in a very buoyant material, if you could get something hard enough. That would give you an instant mounted pop-up.

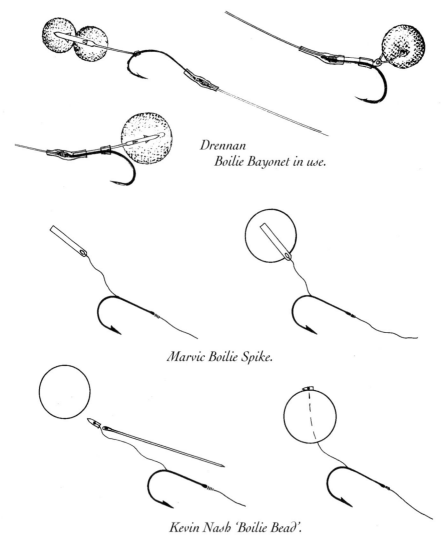

Drennan
Boilie Bayonet in use.

Marvic Boilie Spike.

Kevin Nash 'Boilie Bead'.

1. Push bead through bait using blunt end
*   of a fine needle.*

2. Turn bead to lay flat on bait and
*   pull hair tight.*

Again on similar lines is the Kevin Nash hair bead. This is a tiny hollow plastic bullet-shaped bead which is tied to the hair, then pushed through the bait on the end of a needle. When it emerges on the other side, it is turned to lie flat on the bait, and so stops it coming off.

HOOK TIGHT TO BAIT

As more and more carp were caught on the hair, so the fish began to learn ways round it. Their normal habit of sucking and blowing at food probably allows them to get away with mouthing baits far more often than we realise. Anglers began to get runs, but on striking failed to make contact, sometimes retrieving a bait-less hair. It seemed the carp were moving off with the bait between their lips, and not getting the hook into their mouths. Once again anglers began moving the bait nearer to the hook in an effort to ensure that if a fish picked the bait up it would get the hook. A return to the old side hooking rigs would have seemed an obvious thing to do, but it was now realised that these had two major disadvantages. Firstly the hook made a large hole in the bait, allowing the easy entry of water, and secondly, side-hooked baits were prone to swivelling around on the hook-shank, and masking the hook point. New rigs were invented to ensure the fish would get the hook into its mouth when it picked up the bait, and that the bait would not swivel round. One of the earliest was the much publicised 'looney rota' rig, originating on the banks of Savay.

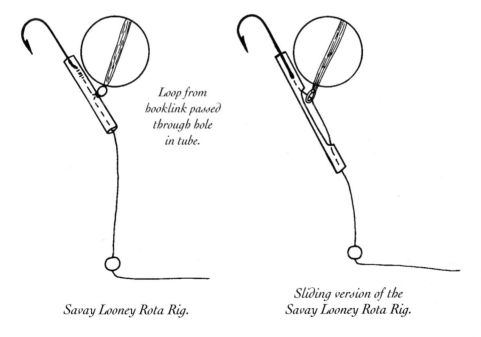

Loop from hooklink passed through hole in tube.

Savay Looney Rota Rig.

Sliding version of the Savay Looney Rota Rig.

Two beauties for Gary Bond on the bent hook rig.

The lovely linear (left) weighed 19.12 and the clonking mirror (below) 33.12.

More recent developments are what has now become known as the swimmer rig, and the bent hook. The latter deserves a special mention because it is probably the most significant advance in rigs since the original hair. It has been known for some time that carp were picking up baits, and moving away, or 'backing off', checking for resistance. Instead of panicking into a run, it seemed the carp on feeling resistance, were in many cases getting rid of both bait and hook. With the standard hook, this was often easy for them to do, as it would sometimes slide over their lips sideways, and not stick in. The shape of the bent hook causes it to flip round and dig in as soon as it comes across the carp's lips. This is easily demonstrated by the well known 'finger test' where you tie a bent hook onto a short length of line, and draw it slowly across an extended finger. If the hook is bent in the right place, which is about $1/3$rd of the way down from the eye, it will flip round and dig in every time. Once in, the shape of the hook causes it to become firmly embedded when pressure is applied, the direction of pull being directly in line with the hook point. Some anglers have experienced difficulty in removing such hooks, and if this is the case I advise you to cut the hook up with wire cutters rather than damage the fish.

The most useful sizes would seem to be 4 or 6, and you can now buy commercial patterns, or bend your own using long shanked fly-tying hooks. Remember, for best effect to use hooks with a down-turned eye. There are now variations on the original bent hook rig, which had the bait tied to a small look positioned at the point where the hook was bent. Anglers are now tying hairs on the bent hook, in various places, and Jim Gibbinson has come up with a hook aligner, a very short piece of tubing attached over the eye of a standard hook, the line emerging from a small hole in the side of the tubing, below the hook eye.

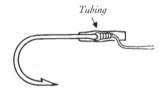

Jim Gibbinson's hook aligner.

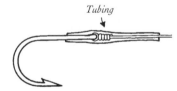

Alternative "aligner".

This apparently causes the hook to flip round like a bent hook. I may be doing something wrong, but I cannot make this hook aligner perform as efficiently as a bent hook. It does flip round, but not ALL the time. It seems that the function of the tubing is to make a straight eyed hook behave like a down-eyed hook. I assume the reason for not using a down-eyed hook in the first place is that there aren't any carp hooks with a down eye. Anyone like to make one? I have been able to make a normal hook flip round like a bent hook by attaching a longer (½inch) piece of flexible tubing over the eye and threading line through it in the normal manner. The principle would seem to be that if a hook is coming out of a carp's mouth, a jolt as the eye, or in this case tubing, hits the fish's lips will cause it to flip over. This is however dependent on there being enough of the hook left in the mouth to perform this function, which is why long-shanked hooks work better than short-shanked ones. Much of this is theory, as the attachment of a bait can change things considerably.

I don't know how the swimmer rig got its name, but I do know it was in use for some time before it actually acquired that name. The rig is set up using an up-eyed hook, and the bait is fixed tightly to the back of the eye. The bait must be tight to the eye and not allowed to swivel round and mask the hook-point.

Two good ways of doing this are to use elastic, or power gum to attach the bait, or to pass a loop of the hook-link through the eye and tie the bait to that. When the hook-link is tensioned, the bait will be held tight to the eye. If you want extra insurance, cut the point off a small pin, and push this through the eye and into the bait. Be aware though that this will allow a small amount of water to seep into the bait, and will eventually affect its buoyancy.

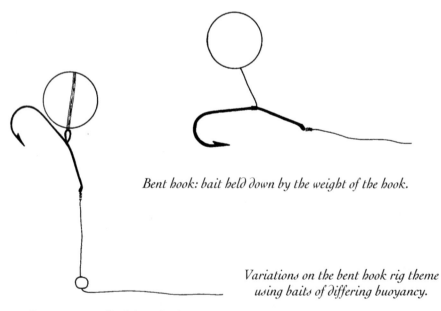

Bent hook: bait held down by the weight of the hook.

Variations on the bent hook rig theme using baits of differing buoyancy.

Pop-up on standard bent hook.

Basic bent hook rig using spare end of knot and tubing to form loop.

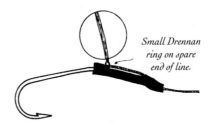

Small Drennan ring on spare end of line.

Bent hook using sliding arrangement.

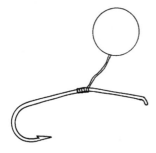

Bent hook and hair rig.

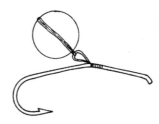

Dental floss loop whipped to shank.

Bent hook and 'D' rigs.

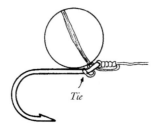

Swimmer rig: Bait tied on loop made with spare end of knot.

Swimmer rig using hook-link loop through eye to tie bait on.

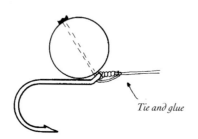

Tie and glue

Swimmer rig: Bait held on with power gum.

Variations on the Swimmer Rig theme

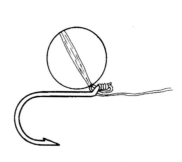

Swimmer rig: Bait tied to loop made from hook-link.

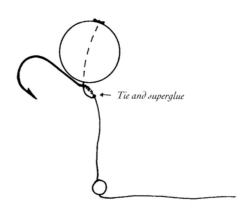

Tie and superglue

Swimmer rig using power gum to affix bait.

LENGTH OF HOOK-LINK

Any one of the above methods of mounting a bait on a hook can be fished in many different ways, and with any of a large variety of hook-links. Again, starting with basic principles, the shorter the hook-link, the more likely you are to make the fish bolt. Very short hook-links are intended for that purpose, so the fish will feel resistance almost immediately, and panic. This is a useful ploy when fishing mass baits such as hemp, where you would not expect the fish to move very far between picking up each mouthful of food. Short hook-links should also prevent bite-offs in this situation, and for maximum effect are best fished with heavy fixed leads. Most anglers I see nowadays use hook-links of 9-12 inches. Though I can see this is a good length to choose, I can't help thinking if everyone is doing that we are getting a little predictable!

The length of the hook-link should be dictated largely by the behaviour of the carp you are trying to catch, and in some cases can be critical. It is a good idea to start fishing a water with different length hook-links on each rod, adjusting each according to the action you are getting. If for instance you are getting runs on short hook-links, but not hooking the fish, or losing them with the hook pulling out, a change to a longer hook-link may make a difference. If on the other hand you are using long hook-links, and know fish are on the baits, but are only getting twitches, or no action at all, using a shorter hook-link might help. Always note the position of a hook in the carp's mouth. If it is on the outer edge of the lips, it may be beneficial to use a longer hook-link; if it is some way back, you might want to try a shorter one.

It is not much good using a 2 inch hook-link if the bottom of the lake is comprised of 2 feet of thick silt, unless of course you think the carp are feeding exclusively on items of food deep within the silt, and judge it to be a good place to present the bait, in which case, think about what bait you are using - I doubt a boilie would be much good in this instance. If the carp are sucking at baits from 9 inches away, make sure your hook-link is long enough to allow the bait to reach them. Be aware that pulling back after casting may effectively shorten the hook-link, depending on where the carp is when it attempts to pick the bait up. This is illustrated in the Diagram on page 78.

Some consideration must be given to baiting patterns. A carp will generally have to move much further between each bait if you are using boilies, than if you are using particles. Fishing long hook-links over a bed of hemp is asking for bite-offs.

There is a relationship between the type of hook you use, and the length of the hook-link. The shorter the distance between the hook and lead, particularly where heavy leads are used, the more downward pressure will be exerted on the hook. In extreme circumstances, a short hook-link when used in conjunction with a straight or out-pointed hook, the tearing action of which has already been mentioned, may cause the hook to pull out. Again I say this may only happen in extreme situations, but the use of a hook with an in-turned point may help prevent it pulling out.

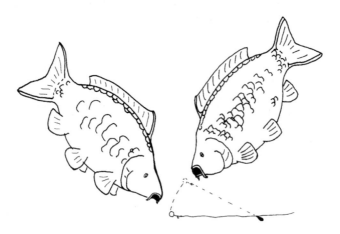

First carp sucking at bait on fully straightened hook-link; bait won't reach fish's mouth. Second carp can suck bait up, though tight hook-link may prevent bait from entering mouth properly.

'Wildie' type carp

Big gravel pit mirror carp.

Some fish may have to up-end further to get at the bait than others.

Long hook-links are more likely to tangle, so if you want to use a long hook-link it is probably best to use an extending one, which can be P.V.A.'d up for casting. These can be very effective, and if set up correctly are one of the few arrangements which can allow a carp a fair amount of movement with the bait without encountering any resistance at all.

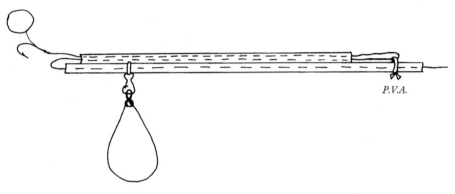

Extending hook-link using double tubes glued together.

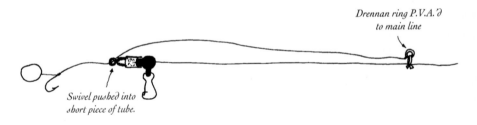

Drennan ring P.V.A.'d to main line

Swivel pushed into short piece of tube.

Extending hook-link set up without tubing.

You can fish a buoyant bait anywhere between the bottom and the surface, and I know of carp that have been caught on baits fished 5 feet from the bottom in 7 feet of water. There is nothing strange about this; if carp are consistently cruising just 2 feet below the surface, then that is a logical place to present a bait. You can do this by fishing a normal length of hook-link, and letting line out so the bait rises to the required depth.

This can be achieved either by measuring out the line you have paid, or letting the bait rise to the surface, then pulling it back down for a couple of feet. To do this, especially at range, where the bait will have to pull a considerable weight of line through the lead, unless you use a float of some kind, the bait itself will have to be very buoyant, and it may be better to fish a 5 foot hook-link, which can be bunched up and tied with P.V.A. before being cast out.

John Read with a 29lb+ mirror taken on a hair rigged boiled bait.

Left. John Miles with an upper twenty taken on a critically balanced hair rigged bait.

Below: Alan with a particle caught big double.

TYPE OF HOOK-LINK

Some hook-link materials, such as Kryston Silkworm and Supersilk are just above neutral buoyancy. If you don't pull these back a bit after casting, they may float above the hook, or in the case of pop-ups, may be hovering around it. If you examine the photographs on page 83 which illustrate various hook-links and rigs in water, you will note that many of the hook-links do, to some extent, hover above the lake bed. All these pictures were taken after the hook-links had been allowed to soak for two hours, and all were left to lie more or less where they had fallen in order to assimilate the angler not pulling back and straightening the hook-link after casting. In theory this presents a potential for a tangle; in practice it doesn't seem to happen, though it will sometimes tangle as you reel in. You should note that critically balanced baits will probably be moved around by any currents present, even slight movements caused by fish passing near baits, and the hook-link may be pulled straight by this action whether you require it or not. If you are concerned about how your hook-link may behave when in water, you can try it out in your bath.

There are many different types of very supple hook-links available now, and in terms of what the fish may feel as it picks up the bait, there is probably little to choose between the best ones. If you think the carp are dropping the bait because they can feel the line, then multi-strands are the best hook-links to use.

Below view of various hook-links when immersed in water.

If you are using supple hook-links, which I would guess most of you are, then you are going to have problems with tangles. I've covered the basics of that already, in the sections on anti-tangle aids, and tubing. If you are using multi-strand, Kryston No-Tangle is excellent. I also alluded to the helicopter rig earlier, and this has been very effective in preventing tangles. It is set up as in the Diagram, the swivel being free to rotate around the tubing. You can use fine tube, heavy line or lead-core fly-line to set this rig up. The two stops are adjustable, so you can move the hook-link away from the lead if you are fishing over silt, or weed. Terry Eustace includes the main part of the rig (minus hook-link), ready made up on neat $\frac{1}{2}$mm tube in his Gold Label range. You can buy the 'swivel and bead' bit from John Roberts, fitted onto a short rubber sleeve to which you attach whatever length of tube you require.

The author and a 19+ caught on a big hook / short hair set up.

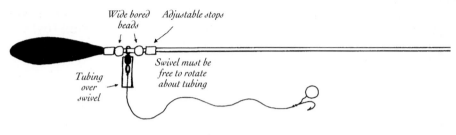

Wide bored beads *Adjustable stops*

Tubing over swivel

Swivel must be free to rotate about tubing

Helicopter rig.

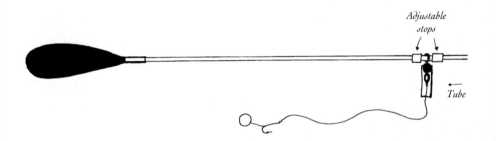

Adjustable stops

Tube

Fixed paternoster – swivel fits tightly over tubing.

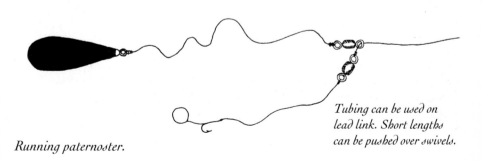

Running paternoster.

Tubing can be used on lead link. Short lengths can be pushed over swivels.

LEADS IN THE RIG

For most carp fishing needs a fairly standard arlesey bomb will suffice, though we have already mentioned the benefits round leads and the Kevin Nash bolt leads may offer in a fixed lead set up. The choice here is up to the angler - I doubt there is much to choose between them. If you are fishing over silt, where you don't wand the lead to sink too far, or over snags where you want the lead to rise quickly in the water when you reel in, I strongly recommend you use tri-lobe type leads, or the Eustace Buzz bombs. Even in the large sizes, they perform these functions very well.

I have mentioned the comet type leads, and I think the only advantage they may give is in casting distance. The fact that they lie flat and generally have stiffish tubing passing through their centre may help prevent them becoming caught up on gravel bars.

For practical fishing purposes the main choice is whether to fish a big lead, or a small one, and whether to fix it, or let line run through it. In between is the back-stopped rig, which allows a certain degree of movement before the lead is felt, and the back-stop may be positioned at any reasonable distance behind the lead. In so far as size of lead goes, I doubt there is any great advantage in using small ones, unless you perhaps want to cast to a fish without alarming it. The resistance offered by a big lead in a free running set up is probably no greater than that offered by a small one; indeed the smaller lead may create a more uneven resistance by dragging across the bottom, and catching up here and there. The fixed lead set up will not work efficiently with small leads. The more wary the carp become, the bigger the lead you will need to ensure the hook pricks the fish to the extent of making it run. Carp anglers are using leads as heavy as 6oz to achieve this. It may not be necessary to use leads that heavy on your water - you will have to judge for yourself. It will depend to a great degree how much pressure the fish have been under from anglers. I have heard of a carp picking up a bait and very sharp hook, lifting a 3oz lead from the bottom, then lowering it down again and getting rid of the hook, all this with no indication at the rod. And this was a carp that had probably never been hooked in its life. Food for thought!

If you are fishing at long range you will have trouble in offering a resistance-free rig, as in order to move your indicators, the carp will have to move a considerable amount of line first. If you can't do away with resistance almost totally, then I think it best to go in the other direction and offer as much resistance as practically possible. Clipping the line up tight, or using the fixed lead is probably the most efficient in this case, and with the right length of hook-link should work in most situations. Don't forget though that when using heavy fixed leads, or tightly clipped lines, you will only get indications from hooked fish, and may not know if a fish is testing your bait. Of course, you may not know that with other rigs, but using running leads, or back-stops gives you more chance of spotting those twitches. The trouble is, if you then get a 3 inch lift that stops, you will probably tell yourself that it would have been a run had you fixed the lead, or clipped up! You can sometimes see these small indications by watching the rod-top and I'm surprised no-one has yet quiver-tipped for carp, especially in winter! I intend to try it myself one day. If you are using a fixed lead, please don't fix it to the line in such a way that, should you break off for any reason, the carp will not be able to get rid of it. Carp can and do get rid of hooks, but if they are towing a 3oz lead around, this may become snagged, tethering the fish. The best way is to push the hook-link swivel into the anti-tangle tubing, so in an emergency the carp will be able to free itself. You could also use a bead and stop-knot behind the tubing, as you would if you were using a back-stop. The advantage of this method is that if you want to change from fixed lead to back-stopped rigs, you can just slide the stop-knot up the line. I find stop-knots are best made from power-gum, as this can be pulled tight without damaging the line. I used to use ledger stops of various kinds, but found unless they fitted so tightly on the line, to the point where they may damage it, they often moved, especially if you got a screaming run when fishing over a muddy bottom, where the lead had sunk in creating a great deal of resistance. Then you could find the stop would slide as much as 10 yards up the line. This may not sound serious, but wait until it jams in the tip ring, with the carp still 30 feet away, and there is no-one to net the fish for you! Power gum stop knots will quite easily pass through the tip ring, if they move at all.

STRINGERS

For those who don't know what stringers are, they are a quantity of baits attached to the end-tackle by a water soluble tape or string, made from P.V.A. They are useful in that they enable you to concentrate free offerings around your hook-bait, and to some extent, help prevent tangles on the cast. If you put a lot of baits on the stringer, you may have to use a smaller lead to avoid over-loading your rod or to enable you to cast any distance. Some anglers thread the P.V.A. through the hookbait as well. I can see this would help prevent tangles, but it also makes the hole in the bait bigger, though I concede the P.V.A. may to some extent block this hole for a while.

Gary Bond returns a twenty plus caught on the Alec Welland rig.

BAITS

Though baits are not strictly the province of this book, they are essentially part of any rig, and whilst I do not intend to go into any detail on their content, I will mention them in so far as they affect a rig.

The obvious choice is whether you are going to fish your bait on the bottom, or off it. This applies not only to boiled baits, but to many particles and other baits, such as luncheon meat, all of which can be made to float. If you are going to fish pop-ups, then you still have a choice of whether your bait will be critically balanced or not. In theory, you can fish either of these methods on any of the rigs in this book, though it will be noted some are more suited to one method than another. A good illustration of this is the previously mentioned example explaining why 'D' rigs and their variations may work better with pop-ups than with bottom baits. In this case, using a pop-up should help ensure the bait stays in the right place and the hook goes in the carp's mouth the right way round. If your hook bait is exactly the same as your free offerings, bear in mind the fish may well detect the weight of the hook, so use the smallest practical size. Making your baits in different sizes can help, meaning the carp has to exert a varying amount of 'suck' on each one. Using more than one hookbait on the hair will also work, the weight of the hook then becoming a lesser proportion of the weight of hook and baits as a whole, and therefore less noticeable. You can also give the hook itself neutral buoyancy by impaling small pieces of polystyrene on it, or using some floating putty. There are rigs that have the hook floating above the bait, ensuring that the hook will always go in first if the bait is picked up.

Critically balanced baits are those that just sink, either by the weight of the hook, or by some form of small weight attached to the line at varying distances from the hook. In the early days of these baits, I would imagine it gave the carp quite a shock when they applied the amount of suck required for a free offering to one of these neutral buoyancy baits. The baits must have flown into their mouths, and probably caused them to bolt. Now though, this may be something a carp can use in its defence. Imagine a carp coming across your baits, and fanning them up with their pectorals to see which ones are tethered. The critically balanced bait may float around for some time, while all the safe ones sink quickly to the bottom! If they learn as fast as some people think they do, they'll soon suss that one out. Non critically balanced baits, plus the hook, should be at least as buoyant as the hookbaits. I am at a loss as to why carp fall for the most obvious trick, the pop-up. They keep doing it though, don't they? I think that much of the time the carp don't even realise the bait is off the bottom.

The hair rig has been used to great affect with very hard baits. The logic behind this is that a fish will have to take a hard bait back into its throat teeth in order to crush it and will, therefore, have to take in the hook as well. Soft baits may be sucked without the hook entering the carp's mouth at all.

A very successful method of fishing is to use two baits on the hair, a buoyant one, which is countered by a non-buoyant one. There is, of course, no reason why you should stop at using two baits. As long as you are not using really big baits, strings of as many as six baits, being a mixture of buoyant and non-buoyant, have caught fish. You could also use more than one hair, putting one or more baits on each.

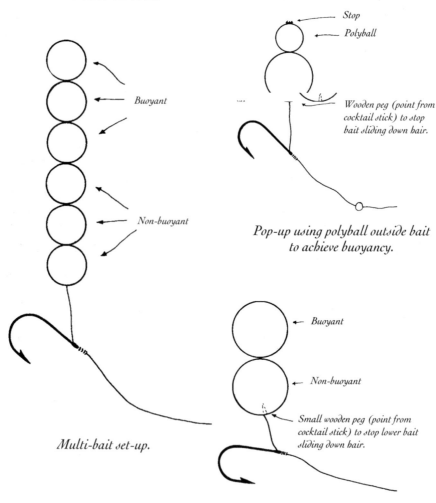

Stop

Polyball

Buoyant

Wooden peg (point from cocktail stick) to stop bait sliding down hair.

Non-buoyant

Pop-up using polyball outside bait to achieve buoyancy.

Buoyant

Non-buoyant

Small wooden peg (point from cocktail stick) to stop lower bait sliding down hair.

Multi-bait set-up.

Non-buoyant bait counteracts buoyant bait giving neutral buoyancy overall.

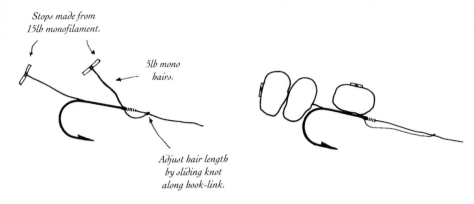

Stops made from
15lb monofilament.

5lb mono
hairs.

Adjust hair length
by sliding knot
along hook-link.

Multiple particle rig: stops are permanently attached to hairs.

As I said, I don't intend going into detail on baits, but briefly, you can make them buoyant in several ways, and some are more suited to one type of bait than others. You can microwave them, grill them, cook them in the oven or fry them. Both particles and boilies can have buoyant inserts inside them, the boiled baits at the time of making. Both particles and boilies can be 'drilled' out on the bank, where they can have polystyrene or rig foam inserted. As an alternative to making the bait itself buoyant, you can just attach a buoyant material such as a polyball or a piece of rig foam to the hair. This doesn't seem to put the fish off, though they may wise up to it. I know of anglers who have caught carp on hair-rigged pieces of cork fished over a bed of tiger nuts. The polyball or foam is best attached above the bait, so it keeps the bait up in the water. If you find the bait keeps sliding down the hair, you can peg it in place using the small point from a wooden cocktail stick. This will expand when wet, and help keep water out of the bait.

FLOATERS

Rigs, that is hook, hair and hook link, can be much the same for floater fishing as for bottom fishing. The hair rig and bent hook will both work. A friend of mine who has caught large numbers of fish on floaters, swears by the 'looped' hair, as illustrated on below.

Another good method when using the hair is to make the hook float, and for the fly tiers amongst you, this is easily achieved with a dubbing of seal's fur or something similar, well impregnated with a good floatant. The most basic way of presenting a floater is to free-line it, and if you can reach the fish with this method, it is almost as good as any other. I say almost, because even if you manage to cast a free-lined floater any distance, any amount of surface movement will put a bow in the line and make the bait move at an unnatural angle. Use of a controller will help prevent this. I have already mentioned the Gardner suspenders, which help keep the line off the surface whilst still allowing the bait to move.

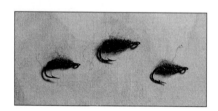

*Bent hook with double elastic loops
to hold floaters.*

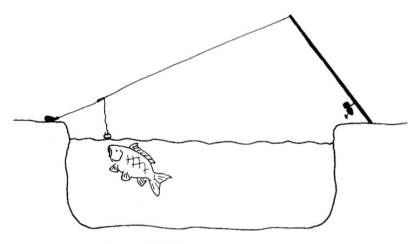

1. Fishing narrow waters.

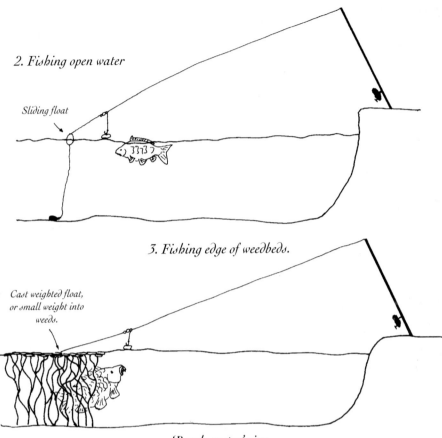

2. Fishing open water

Sliding float

3. Fishing edge of weedbeds.

Cast weighted float, or small weight into weeds.

'Beach-caster' rigs.

Another method of keeping line off the surface, but this time not allowing movement of the bait, is the Beachcaster rig. The basic principle behind this was first mentioned by Dick Walker in 'Drop Me A Line', and now that excellent book has been reprinted, I expect many of you will also have seen it there. The variations of this rig can be seen in the diagrams on these two pages.

If you are not using the hair, then it is a good idea to make a small elastic loop on the hook and fasten the bait by this means. It makes changing the bait very easy indeed. A good elastic to use is knicker elastic, especially the flat sided stuff - and obtaining it could have its little bonus!

So far as hook links go, for floater fishing where wary fish are being pursued, I would strongly recommend you use multi-strand which, when in water, is virtually undetectable. Hook links of 2 feet or more in length can also be advantageous.

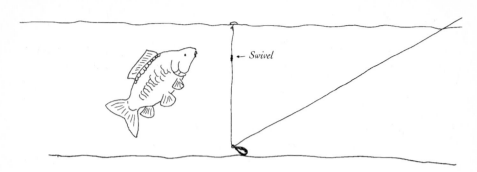

Basic tethered floater rig.

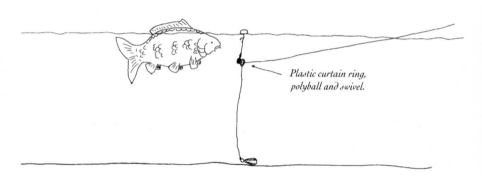

Alternative tethered floater rig.

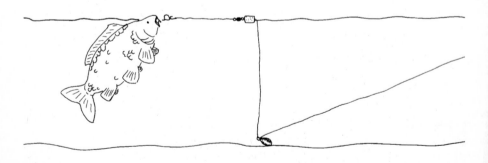

Tethered floater using bored out wine bottle cork.

FLOAT FISHING

I almost forgot float fishing! It really comes under fishing methods, which this book is not intended to cover in any detail. The only parts of a rig which apply to float fishing are the hook link and hook/hair. Basically, anything you can fish on a ledger, you can also fish on a float. One should though, err on the side of the confidence rigs such as the hair and its variations. Bent hooks and the like are really intended to be fished in conjunction with a bolt rig and I don't see the point of putting a fixed 6oz lead on a float! There can be some advantage though in using modern hook link materials such as silkworm and multi-strands.

I mentioned previously that carp are sometimes caught by fishing a bait at varying depths. Using a float is obviously an excellent method of presenting a bait to sub-surface cruisers, though I must admit I haven't tried it; nor do I know of anyone who has caught any number of fish doing so. It is, however, a method to commit to memory, and though you may feel a bit silly fishing in such a manner, it might just catch you the odd fish on one of those hot summer days when carp are cruising around just under the surface. The best type of float to use is a large waggler, with a big sight-bob. I wonder if you could catch them on an E.T. drifter...?

Gary Bond returns a 22.06 mirror caught on the Alec Welland rig.

This picture. 21.10, first of 2 20's taken in an hour on critically balanced boilies. Below. 25.12 caught on a side hooked bean and a cane Mk. IV.

PRACTICAL APPLICATIONS

I don't think it possible to cover every possible variation in a carp's behaviour and relate it to all the possible combinations of rigs which anglers may use. What I will do is to give some examples of known carp behaviour, and try to describe the rigs which could be used in each case.

The question of whether to use fixed, free-running or back-stopped leads is one that will be dictated by various factors, which should be known to the angler. I can't tell you what rig to use on your water, but what I will try to do is get you thinking about the rigs you are using.

Carp sucking and blowing at baits

Before some know-all takes me to task, let me begin this section by saying that carp don't actually 'suck' baits up. What they do is close their mouths, then expel the water therein through their gills, thereby creating a vacuum in their mouth. When the mouth is opened again water, and any objects light enough to do so, rush in to fill that vacuum. For the purpose of this book I have referred to that action as 'sucking'.

This is particularly common behaviour in fish, and they tend to suck and blow at all kinds of odds and ends, not just baits. It is a basic behaviour pattern, and one that the angler must be aware of. They don't always do it of course, otherwise very short hook-links wouldn't work. I don't know what governs whether or not carp will suck at baits, nor the distance from which they will do so. It seems logical that the murkier the water, the less the distance they are likely to be sucking from. The converse may not apply though.

It also seems unlikely they would be sucking up baits from a great distance at night. If carp are behaving in this manner then, as I have already mentioned, the length of your hook link should be carefully considered. A standard hair rig, or one of the sliding ones would probably be more likely to catch up than a rig which has the bait tight to the hook.

Whether you use fixed, free-running or back-stopped leads will depend on other factors and I don't think any one of them is better than another in this situation. I hope by now that I've given you enough information for you to be able to make that choice yourself.

Carp picking up bait from the bottom.

To pick up, rather than suck up a bait from the bottom, a carp must, to some extent, up-end. In order to get their mouth to a bait, short, fat fish will have to tilt into a more vertical position than long thin ones, which might be a worthwhile consideration if your lake is full of wildies!

Sometimes, carp will stay in this vertical position whilst moving on to other baits, while at other times they return to the horizontal. Hair rigs do work in this situation, but educated carp may move off with the hook outside their mouths. Any one of the rigs where the bait is close to the hook will give you a chance of hooking these fish. A fixed lead and shortish hook link can be very effective with these rigs, especially if the length of the hook link is such that it is fully straightened as the carp moves back to a vertical position, jolting the hook into the fish's bottom lip. Hooks should be very sharp, and it is worth mentioning that a small hook will go in more easily than a big one.

I've never seen it myself, but I have heard of carp up-ending over baits, pushing their mouths tight to the bottom around the bait and 'sucking'. Any bait attached to line will obviously not move, the line being trapped between the lake bed and the carp's mouth. While I find it hard to believe a carp could actually perform this test, let alone 'think' it out, there is a rig involving double tubing (Page 79) which has been designed specifically to overcome this, and which may proves useful as an extending hook link rig.

Carp 'backing off'

This is a behaviour pattern that appears to have evolved as a response to use of the fixed lead, the fish picking up the bait then moving slowly away. Any sign of resistance and they either eject the bait on the spot or, if the hook is caught up, instead of panicking, return to the spot where they picked up the bait and somehow work the hook out.

Sometimes the hook may just pull out of the mouth whilst the fish is moving away. Using a heavy fixed lead, the angler would have no indication that this was happening, and I suspect it happens an awful lot. The bent hook was designed to counter this behaviour, flipping round and digging in the fish's mouth as the line tightens. I can't see that it would make it any more difficult for the fish to then get rid of the hook, but it may be that the action and shape of the bent hook causes it to get a better hold in the first place. It certainly catches a lot of fish!

One might, of course, hook these fish if a running lead was used, but then we would all have to go back to hitting twitches, wouldn't we?

Long range/short range

At extreme range it will always be difficult for the angler to set the hook himself, due to the amount of stretch in the line. For this reason, fixed or back-stopped leads are best used at long range. Clipping the line tight will also work, but the line may spook the fish. At close range you might prefer to dispense with anti-tangle tubing, unless you feel it is acting in a beneficial way by disguising the line.

For margin fishing, it is best that you fish with a slack line and keep it as close to the bottom as possible, so it won't alarm the fish. You may need to back-lead the line to do this efficiently. This can desensitise the rig and it might be best to use a fixed or back-stopped lead.

Type of bottom: hard/soft/mud/silt/weed

The type of bottom over which you are fishing may have some bearing on your rig. If the bottom is hard, then any rig you judge will fool the fish can be used. When fishing over soft silt, assuming you don't want to actually fish the bait in the silt, then it is usually better to fish a buoyant bait that will sit on the silt, or a pop-up just above it. If you are having to fish in weed, consider that, with a hair-rigged bait, the hook may become caught in the weed, making it difficult for a fish to pick up the bait. Again, using a pop-up will help. If you are using stringers, in this case it is best to tie them up the line somewhere; if you tie them to the hook, they will pull into the weed and it may stick there.

If you are trying to position your bait in a small, clear spot in a weedy area, it may not be possible to do so accurately, even with the use of marker floaters. In this instance, it is a good idea to PVA either a buoyant material or, to avoid having bits of cork and polystyrene floating all over weedy lakes, a spare and very buoyant bait to the hook, then when you cast out this will keep the hook off the bottom until you have pulled the lead onto the clear patch, which you will be able to feel through the rod. An added advantage is that the buoyant material will then float to the surface as the PVA melts, giving you a marker to aim free offerings at. You'll have to be quick if it's windy though.

On lakes with very soft and deep silt, you should be careful about using heavy leads as they may sink several inches into the bottom. I used to fish a lake where, after casting a 1½ ounce lead some 30 yards, you would have to bend the rod double to pull the lead from the silt. Terrific for bolt rigs, but not so good if you are trying to fish without resistance. In this case, it is best to put the lead on a long link, or use a paternoster of some kind. If you are using a long link to the lead, it can be useful to thread a buoyant material on the link, leaving it free to slide up to the main line, thereby ensuring the line is kept out of the mud. A small piece of cork with a hole through it will suffice.

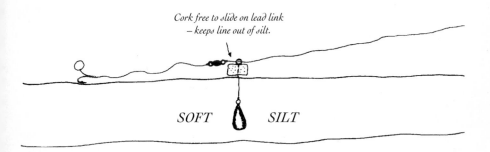

*Cork free to slide on lead link
— keeps line out of silt.*

SOFT   SILT

Size of water

The size of water will not affect your rig so much as your fishing methods. On a very small water, it may be that tight lines will spook the fish, as they may not be able to avoid them. In this case, try to get your line lying on the bottom. This can be achieved with the use of back-leads, or just by pulling the line from the reel and using light indicators.

If you are fishing with slack lines, especially at night when you can't watch the line for movement, it is generally best to use a fixed, or closely back-stopped lead, as the fish will have to move the bait some distance before anything registers on your indicators, and by the time you have been given enough warning to strike, it could be too late. The fixed or back-stopped leads should help set the hook for you.

Clarity

If your water is very clear, then it will probably give you more confidence to fish using inconspicuous end tackle. To this end, consider a hook link which matches the bottom colour, or multi-strand which is almost invisible in water. Consider using camouflaged leads and tubing (if any) and small hooks. The fish will be able to see the baits from some distance, so they may be 'sucking' at them from up to a foot away. Bear this in mind when deciding on the length of your hook-link. Also bear in mind that all this will change when it gets dark!

Depth

The only considerations here are how much light is reaching the bottom of the lake, which is also related to clarity, and the fact that in deep water, you may have a lot more line off the bottom than in shallow water. I don't intend saying any more on that, but just wanted to make you aware of it.

Time of year

In winter, carp generally move around far less than they do in summer and, when they do move, being affected by the low water temperatures, they will often move around in a much more sedate manner than they do in summer. The carp angler should be aware of this and set his rigs so that they will be effective in those circumstances. A shortish hook-link and a very sharp hook fished on a bolt rig can be very effective in winter.

Size of fish

The main consideration here is in the length of the hair. Realistically, most people do not fish for carp that are not capable of taking a hook as large as a size 2/0 into their mouths, so hook size is not a factor to be taken into account here. The length of the hair has already been mentioned, but I should say that this can also depend on where the hair is attached to the hook. If it is attached to the eye, when related to the distance between a carp's lips and its pharangeal teeth, it can be longer, by the length of the hook, than if it were attached to the top or bottom of the bend.

Number of fish - pressured/non pressured

This really relates to how easy your water is. If it is a well stocked and hungry water, then there is probably no need to go in for any great deal of sophistication when setting up a rig. There will probably be a fair amount of competition for food, and most of the rigs will work. On such a water you should get enough action to make any necessary adjustments.

At the other end of the scale, on the hard waters containing few fish, where you may only get one or two takes a year, then I would go in with the very latest rig that is designed to ensure a pick up is converted into a hooked fish.

I know some people say, don't go in on the latest rigs too early, and on some waters I can see the logic in that, but if you are on a water where you expect only one or two takes a year, you will want to make the best of them, more especially if your fishing time is limited.

If you are fishing for carp that have never been fished for, then once you get them onto the baits, you could probably get away with the most basic of rigs. It would be a good idea to do so, as long as you weren't in the situation described above. Once the carp become educated, you always have another rig to turn to. If you go straight in on the hair-rigged bent hook, once the fish wise up to it you may find them very difficult to catch.

Soft and hard mouthed fish

I have fished waters where I have lost a large number of fish due to the hook pulling out. On some waters, especially soft bottomed ones, where the fish's mouths rarely come into contact with anything hard whilst browsing for food, their lips can be relatively soft, and a hook-hold there will often fail.

What you have to do is to try to set up your rig so that you hook the fish further inside the mouth, and rigs that have the bait close to the hook offer the best chance of achieving this. Longer-than-normal hook links will also help, as will larger hooks if you can get away with it. Using a hook with an in-turned point will also be useful, as it is generally accepted they have less of a tearing action.

Conversely, some gravel pit fish have very tough mouths, hardened by a lifetime of browsing over gravel bars and hard bottoms. It can, at times, be difficult to get a hook to penetrate the lips and, again, it is often better to aim for a hook hold further back in the mouth. It is crucial in this case that your hook be as sharp as you can make it and, if you are using a fixed lead, I would go for a big one.

Weather

Weather won't affect what rigs you use, but may affect your fishing method which will, in turn, dictate which rig you should use on any given day.

On a calm, sunny day you can do what you like. However, if you are trying to fish without resistance, you will find it quite difficult in a big wind, especially when there is a strong undertow. In this case it may be better to go for maximum resistance and fish the fixed lead, or clips. In high winds it is often difficult to detect takes other than runs, and in this case the fixed lead (or tightly clipped up line) will give you the best chance of a fish, which picks up the bait, being hooked.

John Read with an October 30lb+ fish caught on a hair rigged particle.

SUMMARY

Well, that's about it. I have tried to cover everything but it is important for the carp angler to realise that from the moment he casts out, to the moment he puts the net under a fish, there have been many variables in operation which will have determined his success or failure.

Unless you can watch what the fish are doing, then many of these variables will be beyond your control. Luckily for us, there seem to be quite a few carp around that make mistakes, though undoubtedly our baits are picked up many times without us knowing anything about it. Even the match angler will occasionally retrieve a squashed maggot, having had no indication on the finest of float tackle. A maggot which has been squashed has been all the way back to the fish's pharyngeal teeth and out again!

I hope I have given enough information in this little book to help you to persuade some carp to slip up occasionally. Inevitably, I have not been able to cover every set of circumstances, and may have interpreted some situations differently to the way other anglers would. Some of you may be complaining because I've left something out - that's because I'm not perfect, or anywhere near it! Or perhaps you are still keeping it secret!

Most of the time I have tried to remain objective, and to get you to think about what you are doing, and why you are doing it. I have been careful to leave openings by not using those dangerous words 'always' and 'never' (except where that applies to never permanently fixing leads!).

Gary Bond returns a 22.08 mirror caught on the bent hook rig.

Good luck and good fishing.

I know many anglers think that the successful anglers they read about are using some kind of secret rig. I think the financial incentives for publishing successful rigs are now too tempting for that to be the case! There are many occasions when fish just don't feed; but sometimes they will suddenly switch on, and be caught all around a lake, and every one on a different set up.

Nowadays, all other things being equal, he who fishes longest catches most fish, and with time spent on the water comes experience and, through that, confidence, which is one of the best ingredients there is.

Most of the ideas in this book you will already have seen in print. They are a combination of the thoughts of many carp anglers over the past three decades, but don't think that the first person in print with an idea necessarily invented it - there are many glory seekers around these days!

Don't take anything as being sacrosanct - if you can see a good reason for adapting a rig to your own requirements, then give it a go. As Dylan once said, "Imitation is the basis of originality". But do remember, you don't have to go to the extremes that some anglers do to enjoy your fishing, after all, we are only catching carp and, brilliant angler though he is, 99% of the population have never heard of Rod Hutchinson!

Remember, life moves very quickly - if you don't stop and look around sometimes, you'll miss it.

Good luck and good fishing.